The COURAGE *to* BEGIN *Again*

STORIES OF RESILIENCE, COURAGE, AND REINVENTION

The COURAGE *to* BEGIN *Again*

STORIES OF RESILIENCE, COURAGE, AND REINVENTION

Halo
PUBLISHING
INTERNATIONAL

Halo

PUBLISHING INTERNATIONAL

Halo Publishing International
7550 W IH-10 #800, PMB 2069,
San Antonio, TX 78229

First Edition, May 2025
ISBN: 978-1-63765-797-3
Library of Congress Control Number: 2025905127

Contents

Dear Reader,

As both the publisher and a contributor to this powerful anthology, I found myself deeply moved by every story within these pages. Each narrative brought back memories of my own journey and reminded me of the courage it takes to start over—to leave behind a familiar world and begin anew.

The women who came together for this project did so with extraordinary bravery. They opened their hearts and shared some of the most vulnerable and transformative moments of their lives here in Mexico. It takes strength not just to endure difficult times, but to speak them aloud— and even more so to write them down for others to read.

What struck me most as I read each story was the common thread of hope, determination, and reinvention. I saw parts of myself reflected in their experiences, and I believe you will too. Whether you're at a crossroads, contemplating a big decision, or simply trying to make sense of your own journey—especially if you've found yourself in a new place like Mexico—I hope these stories offer comfort, clarity, and inspiration.

Personally, I've never been one to settle for a life of contentment. I've always believed in the power of opportunity and the importance of reinvention. Even after twenty years of living in Mexico, I'm still learning, still growing, and still striving. And I wouldn't trade that for anything.

To the remarkable women who gave life to this book—Patricia Pulido, Camila Ifanger, Marina Dailly, Joli Divon Saraf, Sadia Salam, Elizabeth Lloyd, Maria

Fernanda Rodriguez, and Maria Paula Prieto—thank you. Your honesty and vulnerability are gifts to all who read them.

And to Kirsten—thank you for listening that night at the restaurant when this was just a wild idea. I'm sure you'll agree, now holding this book in your hands, that it was meant to be. These stories are a testament to the strength of the human spirit and will undoubtedly touch many lives.

May these pages give every reader the courage to begin again, whenever and wherever they need to.

With gratitude and admiration,

Lisa M. Umina
CEO & Award-Winning Author

Our Authors

My journey continues, but it's no longer just about surviving. Mexico has become more than just a place on a map; it's where I've found strength, connection, and a deeper sense of self.

Mexico, Mexico, Here I Come!

From Cultural Shock to Adjusting the Internal Clock!

Marina Dailly

The first few hours and days in Mexico City were magical. The vibrant colors, the sounds, the smells, the chanting Spanish-speaking voices. My brain tricked me; it convinced me I was on a long vacation, and I did not mind since I loved every moment.

I fell into the rhythm of Mexico City quickly. Every dining-out opportunity started with a *mezcalita*—oh, that fresh lime taste with the yummy worm salt! Every sip was a reminder of how lucky I was to be here. And then there was the guacamole. I have never tasted such a delicious avocado in my life—so fresh, creamy, and accompanied by the crispy cilantro perfume. But what truly made my heart sing was the *chicharrón* on top of the guacamole. With every bite of that crispy, savory *chicharrón* pork skin, I was in heaven. It is fair to say that Mexico is definitely love at first bite.

For a while, life felt like a never-ending holiday. I wasn't worried about anything; all I had to do was to enjoy each day, savor the flavors, and experience the little joys. And, boy, did I.

The honeymoon phase lasted longer than I expected, but eventually reality clocked in. The reality is that I had moved around and lived in so many countries that I thought it would get easier with every new adventure. However, there was one thing I hadn't anticipated; with every move, my situation and family status was different. When I first move to Switzerland, I was single, young, and the only responsibility I had was to make sure I did not go crazy on the cheese fondue. It was also different when my husband and I moved to Indonesia; we could explore life at our own speed. However, moving to Mexico City was a game changer; my family situation had grown and now included a two-and-a-half-year-old girl born during the pandemic.

My friends and family always find these new experiences glamorous; they see me as a jet-setter. It is true that each move is exciting and an opportunity to experience another country, another culture. It is, however, also a bittersweet experience, just like the *mezcalita*; in order for you to fully enjoy it, you first need to go through the heavy, spicy salted rim. Early on, I realized it all depends on each person's perspective and unique situation—status, experience, identity, family situation, financial condition, children's ages, specific needs of family members, and whether both parents work. So, all these factors need to be considered because they will shape your transition.

Why Mexico City Was a Game Changer

Mexico City offers everything and anything. It is beautiful, colorful, energetic, and full of history, great museums, jazz clubs, music, bars, top restaurants, festivals, and so many amazing food and cultural choices. With all of this, why was I lost, overwhelmed, and struggling to settle down?

At the time I am writing this, I am one year in, and I have just started feeling "settled." Well, actually, even though we found a place right away, our house was not move-in ready for eight months.

So, reflecting on my year, I am now asking myself what made the move to this dream city difficult? I can identify a couple of things, but please remember that this is from my unique perspective as a mother, wife, who works full-time and has a young child who does not attend school all day long, and, not to forget, with limited Spanish-speaking skills.

First, one fact that made settling down in Mexico City challenging was the city itself. Mexico City is the capital, it is a big city, and it is the heart of Mexico. While it is a hub for many foreign nationals, most come from Latin America, the US, and Spain, which gives the city a strong regional identity based on shared language and shared cultural traits —except perhaps some of the Americans and the Brazilians.

This regional focus means the expat community is spread out, without a central "international bubble" like in cities such as Jakarta, New York, or Geneva, where expats often live in specific neighborhoods. Additionally, if you have children in school, even international schools will primarily communicate in Spanish due to the high number of local and regional families. Therefore, if you're and moving from a non-Spanish-speaking background, it's essential to make Spanish a priority for daily life.

Second, loneliness. Even though I am here with my family, I have never felt so lonely and invisible. As mentioned above, Mexico City is a big city, so finding your bearings in the first few months can be difficult. I work from home, so for months, I never had the opportunity to talk to someone beside my family. I find it quite strange that even when taking multiple Ubers, going to the same gym every day for months, eating at the same restaurant across the street, or simply exploring different bars or events, everyone minds their business and exchange small conversation; no one dared make eye contact. It was as if I were invisible. And when, finally, someone had a basic exchange with me, they assumed I was on vacation and wished me well on my trip.

My husband, too, was facing his own struggles in adjusting. While I spiraled into loneliness, he seemed more able to adapt. At least, he went to work every day, met colleagues, and had some external interactions. But I realized the emotional weight of the move was starting to hit both of us differently. He mentioned to me once, "I just need a night out, with the guys, to drink beer and watch football." That was the moment I realized how much we both needed space to connect outside our little family unit. We needed a reset, maybe a hard reset.

The other challenge I faced when settling in Mexico was access to information and understanding how certain things work. Many people assume the difficulty stems from language barriers, but I don't quite agree with that. For me, the real challenge wasn't the language itself but navigating the systems and finding the right information. For example, locating simple, reliable services, like water delivery services, internet providers, or more standard service such as finding a good general practitioner doctor, can be surprisingly difficult. Even after researching or asking for recommendations, getting a response can be a real challenge. To add to the challenge, many websites don't accept foreign cards—really, not even Visa? Yet, strangely, restaurants do! It can feel a bit confusing at first, but over time, I've learned to navigate these quirks and adapt. At first, all the inconsistencies were pretty overwhelming. But over time I figured out how to navigate things. I had to call multiple times because not all service providers are on WhatsApp. If they were nearby, I'd stop by in person to ask questions. In some cases, I'd order online and then pay through Oxxo. It definitely took some trial and error to get everything set up.

You might be wondering why I didn't just open a local bank account right away. The process is a bit more complicated, first you need to get your residency permit. After that, you apply for the CURP code, which is like a social security number here. And that can take a couple of months to complete.

I had moved and settled in different countries before, but Mexico was different. Why? Was it because of the inherent safety issues, so everyone is a bit wary of strangers? Is it because everyone is tired of tourists invading their city? Or is it because I am so different from everyone else with my black skin and curly wild hair. Or simply that people assume they can't communicate with me due to my limited Spanish or their limited English?

The challenges and isolation wasn't just about being far from family and friends. It was deeper than that. I had to confront who I was in this new country. How do you belong when everything feels so different? I started questioning my identity, wondering if I could ever truly fit into this fast-paced, vibrant world of Mexico City. I had to come to terms with the fact that I wasn't just a visitor anymore. I was living here.

What I Wish I Had Known Before Moving Here

Upon reflecting on it now, there are couple of things that I wish I had known before moving here. The first thing I would have done differently is not rush to find a place to live. Taking temporary housing is a great option to know which neighborhood fits your style, your needs, and your family. Mexico City is a big city, and choosing the right neighborhood is crucial for your overall comfort and lifestyle. Different areas offer different products, prices, and connectivity. Proximity to work, school, and essential services is important. For instance, how easy is it to get to and from your usual activities? If it takes you ten to fifteen minutes just to get out of your neighborhood, it will take at least double or triple that to get to your final destination, depending on traffic and how close you are to the main roads.

What I find really useful and very important, once you identify the area in which you think you want to live, is visiting it at different hours of the day. That will reveal vital information about the area. For example, we visited an apartment after 8:00 p.m. to see what the place and the neighborhood were like at night. One of the apartments I really loved had an amazing terrace, but we ultimately decided not to take it. It was in a noisy area, and the building had thin walls, plus most of the neighbors were young and liked to host parties. While there's nothing wrong with that, I quickly learned that in Mexico, people embrace living life to the fullest, and everyone respects that by letting others do the same. In fact, calling the police because of noise is not really the norm, you just don't do it. So, when choosing a place to live, it's really important to think about whether the location and the building fit your lifestyle.

Another thing I wish I had known and prepared for when I first arrived in Mexico City is planning around emergencies, whether it is planning what to do in case of earthquakes, gas leaks, or medical emergencies. Mexico City is prone to earthquakes, so know your building codes and if you are here with your family, including children, you will also need to plan for medical emergencies. I wish I had thought to research before moving, or upon arrival, to Mexico City. Actually, this applies to relocating to any city, to check and log in recommended hospitals, doctors, and pediatricians. As I mentioned, at the beginning I arrived, enjoyed life , and did not take into consideration or properly prepare for these emergencies. After months, when I found myself in different emergency situations, it was too late. I put myself and my family at risk.

Different health issues will arise; it is completely expected. You are in a new environment and being exposed to new pathogens, viruses, bacteria, and your diet has changed I had chronic stomach issues, which most call Montezuma's revenge. As an adult, this is manageable, and you somewhat know what to do. But my child's emergencies made me feel the most vulnerable and stressed I ended up in the hospital multiple times in the middle of the night. I don't usually rush my toddler to the hospital, but extreme situations, where she was losing consciousness, called for it. I had no idea what to do, where to go or how to control the fever anymore. I panicked; I was scared, so we rushed to the closest emergency room.

With my limited Spanish, having to go to the emergency room, explain complex health issues, and make medical decisions was rough. One doctor proposed unconventional things that I did not fully understand. I had to refuse some of the doctor's recommendations, such as taking my two-and-a-half-year-old daughter's blood or pumping out her stomach. I later found out that some hospitals in Mexico operate in a commercial way; they simply run all types of tests to charge you fees. In situations like this, you have to trust your instincts. So yes, it's important to be prepared for emergencies. I eventually found a great pediatrician, and I learned that, in emergencies, it's best for your primary doctor to work with the emergency team. This ensures decisions are made with your child's medical history in mind, leading to the best outcome for your family.

Another thing I wish I had known before moving here is the climate. It can be mild and temperate, forever spring, but when that wind blows or in the evening, I get quite cold. So, it's best to always be prepared with a layered outfit and a jacket on hand for this ever-changing weather. When we first arrived, I was mostly worried about the high altitude —2,240 meters high or 7,350 feet—and whether I would suffer from altitude sickness. Overall, I was fine, but you can become dehydrated very quickly. So I started drinking more than half a gallon of water per day, and that saved me from altitude sickness.

What Helped Me Settle in the City and What I Have Learned So Far from My Experience

It is indeed true that I have lived an intense beginning in Mexico City. There were so many new beginnings: new city, new job with meetings in different time zones, new house, new language. Adapting to all these different new aspects of my life. Whether starting my workdays at 7:00 a.m., or learning a new language, these all requires top discipline, not only in my sleep regimen but also in the time I dedicated to learn. This is highly demanding and it is impossible to tackle all of this at the same time, you will burn out. I attempted to do all that, while my child sometimes woke up at night. No one can achieve all of this on fragmented sleep.

While all these moments were difficult to manage, and still are, it is important to go through the motions, surrender to the experiences, and do everything in your power to integrate but you need to prioritize. Mexico City has a lot to offer, but there is also a lot to instill fear. Do not let this shape your experience here and limit you. Of course, you have to be careful and avoid putting yourself at risk, but do "live" in the city. Honestly, when you resist the process and loneliness sets in, it begins to show on your face—making you appear more grumpy and even less approachable, which makes it harder to connect with others.

How do you begin to "live" in the city? To be honest, when you struggle with the process of settling in, health issues and loneliness kick in; your facial expressions also start showing signs of grumpiness, and you are even less approachable, and less likely to make friends. But I realized that building meaningful friendships was not only important for me, but for my husband as well. It directly impacted our well-being and mental health. It is also not just about making friends but about finding like-minded friends who are interested in sharing similar experiences. While I did meet some people, I struggled to connect with the right ones, which deepened my sense of isolation and made me grow increasingly frustrated with life in the city. The moment I voiced these concerns, that I was starting to feel depressed and wasn't doing well, was probably the moment I felt saved. These words saved me from going deeper into the dark. That was the moment we decided to become intentional about how to get ourselves out of that situation.

The first thing I prioritized was not language but how to fight my loneliness. I started to practice a lot of self-care such as going to the gym, journaling and writing short stories. I also started forcing myself to go out and meet people. I have joined several international women's clubs such as Girl Gone International (GGI) and IWC. The GGI network is global, with a presence in nearly every country. When I moved from Jakarta to Mexico City, I reached out to fellow GGIs to see if they knew anyone in Mexico City, hoping they could help connect me. It's a great way to get started. In fact, I had an initial introduction through a GGI who used to live in Mexico City. She introduced me to her former child's nanny. Although the nanny didn't end up working with us, she turned out to be an excellent connector, helping me find another amazing nanny in the city. This is helpful, as joining events alone can be intimidating because you are not in the mood to start again, not in the mood to answer the same questions—"Where you from?" "What you do?" What...when...where...—especially if you are not fluent in Spanish.

Despite all these efforts, which provided some help, we were still struggling overall. The turning point for me came when we decided to take a break from Mexico City after months of facing different life challenges. We went to San Miguel de Allende. It was again wonderful. I discovered *molcajetes*, great shopping, some nature, and the magic in the voices of the various *mariachi* bands that fill the historic center. Looking at things from the distance was a game changer in terms of adjusting my expectations.

Leaving the city brought some light on all the things I was missing out on and allowed me to reconnect with Mexico. It is weird to say, but when I was not well, not feeling my best, it was hard for me to connect with the city. I was preoccupied by my own short-term need for survival, and I had little mental or physical space for embracing the city and its culture. So, the hard reset I needed was leaving Mexico City for a couple of days. It allowed me to change my attitude toward what I found difficult and highlighted my need to adjust my internal clock and expectations. Being away from the city allowed me to slow down a bit and refocus on what I love not only about Mexico but what I need to be happy and fulfilled.

This trip became the perfect reset button, offering me a new perspective. It helped me realize that my inner strength needed to be fortified before I could truly thrive in this new environment. It wasn't enough to just adapt; I had to connect with my core. I had to build a foundation that would support me through the challenges. I also had to reevaluate what was important to me in this period of my life, to fix my frustrations, and to conquer my biases. These difficult conversations with myself only happen during difficult times and when I am on the verge of collapsing. They do not happen when I am supported and settled; they only come up during disruptive times.

I came to think of settling in Mexico as if I were building a six-legged table—strong, sturdy, and balanced. Each leg was an aspect of my life that I needed to strengthen in order to survive and thrive here.

Leg 1: Saying Yes to New Experiences— Mexico has a way of offering opportunities at every corner. I learned to say yes to all invitations, even if they weren't my cup of tea, just to step out of my comfort zone. I also learned quickly that Mexico City can be so insanely fun and extreme that you will forget to go home. This is not sustainable for me, but the experiences I loved about Mexico and where I connected revolved around the culture and its inner soul. During *Día de Muertos*, I decided to go all-in and celebrate it as all Mexican families do. Getting our faces painted three days in a row really made me connect with the city. I decided to also go to the Jamaica market, which is probably one of the most beautiful markets I have ever seen in my life—the vibrant colors, the smell of all the flowers. You can also find all the treats and the ornaments you need to create your own *ofrenda*. Initially, I decided to decorate our house and build the ofrenda because I find the idea really cool and the marigold flowers vibrant, but I have come to realize how important this celebration is for Mexicans.

One day when I was coming back from the gym, I noticed there were a Coca-Cola and an apple pie on the ofrenda. I could swear it was not part of the ofrenda before I left. How did it get there? My daughter's nanny was working that weekend, so she was at the house. To honor and remember loved ones who have passed away, everyone adds their favorite treats to their *ofrenda*. Since the nanny was away from her house and in our house , she wanted to make sure that her loved one could still be connected to her, so she added to our *ofrenda* their favorite treats. I was really touched by this because we all felt seen.

Leg 2: Reassessing My Values—Living here forced me to reflect on what truly mattered to me, what I wanted to prioritize during this new period of my life. For me, at this point, that was to live a genuine Mexico experience with its own challenges and opportunities, focus on my wellbeing, but also learn to speak Spanish properly so I contribute even to the simplest experiences, like singing along to a *mariachi* song.

Leg 3: Being Flexible—One of the most valuable lessons I've learned since moving to Mexico is the importance of embracing flexibility. From interacting with service providers to navigating cultural differences, I've come to understand that life here often doesn't follow the strict schedules I might be used to. While it was a tough concept to grasp at first—especially coming from a more time-conscious background—it became clear that flexibility is key to managing daily life. For example, if I need someone to arrive for an event or the nanny to be at my house by 4:00 p.m., it's better to plan ahead and set the time earlier, like 3:00 p.m. That way, I account for the unexpected delays, like heavy traffic, and it's much easier to stay calm. Life moves at its own rhythm, with no to stress. I now just go with the flow and enjoy the journey.

Leg 4: Self-Reflecting—Inner reflection is important. I began using time alone for self-reflection. Why was I frustrated? What I considered to be erratic conversations in the beginning are actually not. I now realize that people are just not as interested in their phones as we thought. Coming from Asia, I was used to everyone always being so connected to their phones, everything happening through WhatsApp and chats. Here, if you want a piece of information, you better call. You can see it everywhere. If you go to a restaurant, everyone is having a genuine conversation; no one is on their phone.

Leg 5: Accepting Imperfection—Settling in a new country isn't easy, and I had to learn to embrace the messiness of the process. Not everything will be perfect, and that is okay. This is especially true when you have children. I made bad decisions in the beginning because I wanted to control the outcome of certain things; for instance, looking for a nanny who speaks English. This is difficult. Kids adapt so well, so fast, and they connect with literally everyone. Out of the three of us, my daughter was probably the happiest in this new city.

Leg 6: Building Deeper Connections— I focused on connecting not just with myself and the people but with the culture itself. I learned to listen, to observe, and to appreciate the depth of Mexico's traditions.

One year later, I can say that I do not have all the answers, but I feel settled and have found some peace and a balance that works for me. The struggle to fit in, to make friends, to let go of some of my fears and biases allowed me to find my place in this bustling and vibrant city. It also shaped me into someone emotionally stronger, more adaptable, and more open than I ever thought possible.

My journey continues, but it's no longer just about surviving. Mexico has become more than just a place on a map; it's where I've found strength, connection, and a deeper sense of self. And when I feel as if I am about to get lost, I can find my way through writing or renew my energy by listening to live *mariachis*.

Envision what kind of life
you wish to have. Then
take the necessary steps
to achieve it.

Keep It Moving

Kirsten Harty

I am incredibly grateful to have partnered with Lisa Umina, CEO and founder of Halo Publishing International, to bring this anthology to life. The idea for the book came about during a four-hour dinner in which we reflected on life and shared our experiences as friends. Lisa was one of the first people in my life to genuinely ask how I was doing in Mexico City. Not just whether I liked it, but what I truly wanted, what I missed, and where I saw myself. That conversation was eye-opening. I felt seen and heard. I shed a few tears. This is what sparked the idea of giving other women who have moved to Mexico City a voice to share their stories…of courage, resilience, and reinvention.

In 2012, I moved to Mexico City from Huntsville, Alabama. For the two years prior to our move, my husband had been traveling monthly to Mexico City for work, spending a week there each time. Finally, his company offered us the opportunity to relocate as a family.

Up to that point, I hadn't traveled much abroad, had never been to Mexico, and didn't have any family or friends who lived in Mexico City. Relocating meant leaving my full-time career as a realtor, the place where my son was born, and the community I had grown to love over the past eight years. It also meant living outside of the United States for the first time. But I was no stranger to starting over and embracing a new life. I had lived for eighteen years in New York before moving to Huntsville, Alabama, just a month after our wedding.

On my first visit to Mexico City, I immediately felt its vibrant energy and warm welcome. I grew up in sparsely populated rural Vermont and Upstate New York, but my college years in New York City had prepared me for a city of twenty million people. The weather was beautiful, not too hot or cold. The food was incredibly delicious, and the service was impeccable. I was surprised to learn that the city was very international and boasted over 200 museums.

I still smile when I think about the love and kindness we received at our hotel on our very first day. I had traveled there with my four-year-old son, and the staff was truly excited to meet the wife and son of my husband, who was a frequent guest. To my son's delight, the bellhops gave him a ride on the luggage cart, the housekeeper left him a small toy car as a gift, and the butler brought milk and cookies. Meanwhile, I was treated to champagne and afternoon tea. If their goal was to win us over, they succeeded.

From the first moment of my stay, I had a feeling that moving to Mexico City was the right choice. What I didn't realize then was that a three-year contract would turn into more than a decade, two separate moves to the city, and finally permanent residency.

When I first found out we'd be officially moving to Mexico City, I went into overdrive. I researched schools in the city, watched every YouTube video I could find about Mexico City, started decluttering our home in Alabama, and set up video meetings with a local realtor in Mexico City. There was so much to do, and while it was a bit overwhelming, I was filled with excitement. There was no blueprint, but over the years, I learned many things that helped me adjust to life in Mexico and find happiness.

My Spanish was very basic when we moved. Throughout school, my preferred language of study was French, so I only studied Spanish for the one year. In 2012, it was uncommon for waiters or store employees to speak English. So I decided, after my first visit to Mexico City, that I needed to take Spanish lessons right away. Prior to our official move, I began taking private lessons and have continued to do so on and off over the years.

During my first year in Mexico City, my husband and I went to dinner in *el centro* and then visited a popular jazz bar to listen to music. For some reason, a television crew was in the bar, and they asked to interview me in Spanish. Fueled by liquid courage, I confidently agreed. Once the cameras were on, however, I froze like a deer in headlights and barely muddled through the interview uttering delayed responses. Though I never gave another interview in Mexico, that experience as a newcomer perfectly summed up my approach to living in Mexico City. I was not afraid to step out of my comfort zone, take risks, or laugh at myself.

On one of my visits to Mexico City, I went to a playground in Polanco with my son. An American woman overheard us speaking in English and didn't hesitate to tell me about the Newcomers' Club, now called the International Women's Club of Mexico City. She explained that it was an English-speaking club with hundreds of women from all over the world; its purpose was to help them adjust to life in Mexico City. The club scheduled monthly activities such as museum tours, coffee socials, volunteer work, and family hikes. The members of the club also shared information on doctors, schools, and tailors. As soon as I went back to the US, I paid online for my membership. The club would later become an integral part of my life. I served as its president for one year and the vice president of member services for three years.

Friendships in Mexico City are truly special. You never know who will become an important part of your life, so it's essential to stay open and receptive. Ten years ago, I met a woman visiting from New York City; she later reached out to me about attending a Welcome to Mexico City meeting I was hosting in my apartment. She was considering moving to the city and wanted to learn more about life here. Although she ultimately decided not to move, we became close friends and have visited each other many times over the years.

I have found that the friendships I have made in Mexico City run deep, especially with those who are new to the city. We automatically share a desire for embarking on new adventures, exploring new hobbies, and embracing new cultures. I think it takes a certain kind of person to have the courage to move abroad. For many of us, our families live thousands of miles away, so it is with these new friends that birthdays, holidays, and important milestones are celebrated. These are the friends who have a set of your house keys and whose names are on your child's emergency-contacts list at school.

I don't see my friends who live in the United States as often as I would like, but they are still a huge source of support for me. There are days that I feel lonely or sad about an ailing family member so far away, and invariably I receive a text message or phone call at just the right time. I value and appreciate each one of my friends. They are often my biggest cheerleaders.

Keeping myself in shape physically and pursuing new hobbies have been essential to my mental wellness. Both are much-needed stress relievers. I enjoy trying new workouts, like Krav Maga, salsa/bachata, and Pilates. I even took up running for a couple of years, entering a different race every month, to accomplish something I never thought possible.

Joining different organizations in Mexico is a great way to meet fascinating people of all ages and all nationalities. I am also a big proponent of starting a club if you can't find one. I started both Women Fit4Life, a fitness group for women living in Mexico City, and Sistahs in CDMX, a women's group focused on Black women living in Mexico City.

Living in Mexico City, my biggest challenge has been taking on the role of stay-at-home wife and mother. I am thankful for the benefits that living in Mexico City has afforded the entire family, but going from working full-time to staying at home is an adjustment. My husband travels for work three to four months out of the year, so it was important that I stay home for our son. We made it a priority that one parent was always available for school meetings, doctor appointments, or soccer practices.

From 2012 to 2015, in Mexico City, I had a part-time gift business called Bits N Pieces, which I started with friends. It offered me the fulfillment I missed from working. We hosted monthly events in our homes, selling beautiful handcrafted items like Talavera platters, woven baskets, blown-glass vases, wooden bowls, and marble jewelry. I loved traveling throughout Mexico and talking to the local artisans from whom we purchased. A couple of times, we invited different artisans to attend our three-hour events and bring their wares, such as handmade Oaxacan wool rugs or ceramic pineapples from Michoacan. These shopping events—hosted with mimosas and appetizers, of course—were a fun way to connect with our group of friends.

Throughout the years, I have dedicated time to volunteering in various ways. Giving back to the community that has welcomed my family and me is something I truly enjoy. Through the clubs I have joined, I have helped provide meals and deliver food to the Mexican community, teach English, and make baby blankets for a local hospital. During the pandemic, my son and I worked together to create and distribute blessing bags to those in need across the city.

My favorite weekly activity is having lunch with my family on Saturday. This is our time to check in with each other and decompress from our chaotic weekday schedules. Every week, we choose a different restaurant, arrive about 3:00 p.m., and take three to four hours to enjoy our meal. For the last four years, we have consistently had this "family lunch," and our son knows it is nonnegotiable.

For my husband and me, it has always been vital that our son maintain a strong sense of family. At five years old, he traveled with an airport companion from Mexico City to Florida to visit my mother-in-law over the summer, and he has Skyped with my parents for an hour every Sunday since he was one year old. During our Skype call, we share what our favorite things were for the week, and my son is responsible for asking a follow-up question to show that he was listening.

In December 2015, I learned that we would be moving back to the US. We had already been in Mexico City for almost three and a half years, so we knew this day might come. It was still a bit of a shock, but I was appreciative for the circle of friends I had made. I felt our time in Mexico was well spent; I had taken Spanish lessons, traveled, toured local museums, volunteered in the community, and taken Mexican-cooking classes.

Our repatriation was exciting but intense. We had to buy a new house and two new cars, enroll our son in a local public school, and, for me, find a full-time job after being out of the job market for over three years. The shift from being a stay-at-home wife and mother, supported by a live-in housekeeper and a full-time driver, to balancing a career while chauffeuring my son, cooking, and cleaning was both rewarding and humbling. The experience taught me to never take anything for granted.

When I moved back to the US, there was comfort in returning to a familiar language and culture, but I missed Mexico. There was a void in my spirit that I couldn't explain. I felt as if I no longer fit in the way I used to, and I had to fight the urge to constantly talk about Mexico. It was no surprise that I sought friendships with those who had lived abroad or were well traveled.

After three years of living in the United States, we were told we would have a second chance to live in Mexico City. Even though I had a fulfilling job, lived in a home that I loved, and had made wonderful new friendships, I did not hesitate. The first time we moved to Mexico City, I wanted to explore a new experience. This time, I wanted to move for the opportunities it could afford my son. We looked forward to our son being enrolled again in a private school and receiving a top-notch education. Spanish classes were not offered yet at his public school in the US, so he spoke very little during the three years he attended. A move back to Mexico would ensure that he wouldn't lose his fluency.

For me, finding an apartment and settling back in was easy. Once again, I quickly joined many different organizations to fill my time and reconnect with a handful of friends who still lived in Mexico City. What I struggled with, however, was starting over and reinventing myself.

Leaving a situation in which I was thriving, rather than dissatisfied, came with a feeling of loss.

Moving with a young son is not always easy, but there are things we did to make our son feel involved in the relocation process. For both of our moves, our son was present during our apartment searches. Of course, the final decision was made by my husband and me, but we asked our son what was important to him and if he liked the apartments.

We selected our first apartment in Polanco because it had a safe, secure green space for our son and a pool for his swimming lessons. When we moved back the second time, we joked that the selection was based solely on the fact it was close to his favorite restaurant.

Each time we moved, we allowed our son to pick out artwork for his room with no input from Mom or Dad. He enjoyed the freedom of creating his own space. We loved that he chose a colorful papier-mâché *alebrije* sculpture by an artist at a local park rather than a picture from a chain store. On our second relocation, we bought him two paintings by artists in San Angel—a modern abstract painting and a painting of a dog wearing revolutionary clothing.

It was important to my husband and me that our son be enrolled in sports and hobbies that he enjoyed. His participation helped him to quickly make friends and become confident living in Mexico. Over the years, he has taken karate, swimming, and boxing. He has played on soccer teams each of the ten years in Mexico.

When he was five years old, we asked our son what instrument he would like to play in Mexico City. He had played the piano for two years in the US, but never really had a passion for it. He told us the tuba or the guitar, so we arranged for private in-home guitar lessons. It was easy to find a guitar teacher. In the end, unfortunately, the teacher thought our son was better suited for the drums.

This year, my son graduates from his international British school. He has lived in Mexico for over half his life. He is fluent in Spanish, bicultural, and conversational in French. It's been a pleasure to see him have friends from all over the world and embrace the food and culture of different countries.

I am happy that my son lives his best life in Mexico City. We try to explain to him that many of the privileges he has had growing up in Mexico City are not privileges he would have had if we were still living in the US. It's a balance. I want my child to grow up feeling as if he belongs in every space and can sit at any table.

My son is my greatest success. I am so incredibly proud of him and the young man he has become. My husband and I are confident that we have given him the tools to be successful in life. We are currently in the college-search phase, and we don't know what his final decision will be, but we are happy that he is considering other countries. He has a global mindset and knows that he has the option to study anywhere in the world.

Balance is essential to living in Mexico City. I like to stay busy, and I like to be involved, but there are days I feel tired, drained, and overwhelmed. I am learning that it is okay to take a break and have some alone time. To find what makes me happy. Maybe it's getting a massage, going for a walk, or reading a book. Life anywhere has its ups and downs, its positives and negatives, and sometimes it's both; that's just part of the process. Even though I am always appreciative for my family and friends, I still feel lonely at times. I can be grateful for my life in Mexico City despite the sacrifices we have made as a family, but still grieve at times for what might have been.

Living abroad is not always easy, but it can be very gratifying. It's an opportunity to reinvent yourself and to pursue new interests and hobbies. Be intentional. If you want to make new friends, you must join various organizations and participate in different activities. You must learn to introduce yourself and make small talk with people you do not know. Sometimes it can be intimidating to put yourself out there, but that is how you continue to grow and learn. Envision what kind of life you wish to have. Then take the necessary steps to achieve it.

Keep It Moving!

Starting over in a strange place is a journey that teaches us that the true home is within us. And it is up to us–no one else–to cultivate that home.

From Inner Chaos to Purpose

Camila Ifanger

I t was early morning when I closed the last suitcase. My heart was torn between sadness and hope
as I thought about what awaited me in a country
I barely knew and had often said I would never live in.

In Brazil, we have a saying: "Don't spit in the air, or it
will fall on your face." That's exactly what happened. It
landed squarely on my face.

Two months before that early morning, my husband
locked himself in our bedroom for at least an hour. It
was April 2021, the tail end of a difficult time for the entire
world—the COVID pandemic. A time that brought something
completely unexpected, new, and unpredictable—lockdown.
Lock…what?

The lockdown in Europe was intense and controlling.
For months, we lived without the basic right to come and

go. No leaving the house unless absolutely necessary. No wandering aimlessly on the streets. No meeting people.

But, I must admit, I was privileged. Unlike in many parts of the world, we weren't stripped of the right to schooling. My daughters were able to continue attending classes. Because of that and so many other things we experienced during this time, I rarely complained about the COVID pandemic.

Of course, it was a period of sadness. Without a doubt, it was. But not a time for complaints. Those are two different things. Sadness, yes—for the lives lost, the jobs and opportunities gone, the increase in global poverty, the strain on healthcare systems, and so much more. But complaints and bitterness, no—these were not emotions I carried with me.

For me, there's always a learning opportunity in every situation. Always. No matter how difficult or painful. That's my modus operandi. That's how I've learned to protect myself from the pain and challenges life throws at me. Maturity has taught me to view difficult situations as opportunities to grow. And I can confidently say that this perspective has strengthened my inner world.

Our bedroom became my husband's office for remote work during the pandemic. It was in that very room where something happened…something I was completely unprepared for.

The First Move

We were living in Brussels, Belgium. We'd arrived in January 2020; two months later, the day after my birthday, we were told the country was going into lockdown. I had never even heard that word before.

As a family—my husband; our two daughters, Maria Eduarda and Rafaela, who were eight and six years old at the time; and I—this was our first experience living outside Brazil. We had left behind family, friends, my job as an HR director, emotional stability, and the material comforts we had built during ten years of marriage.

We packed fear, insecurity, and uncertainty into eight suitcases; we would buy whatever else we needed once we arrived in our new country. In those same eight suitcases, we also packed hope—hope for a new family story, new opportunities, new friends, and new languages. We dreamed of new cultural and academic experiences for the girls, the thrill of living near incredible places, and a life full of adventure, travels, and unforgettable family moments. The certainty of these upcoming journeys was the most exciting part of moving far from home. And so, with high expectations, we crossed the Atlantic.

The pandemic caught us off guard, just as it did the rest of the world. We were still in the process of making our rental apartment livable for a fresh start—buying furniture, kitchen utensils, appliances, winter coats, rain gear, and waterproof boots (because, if you don't know, Belgium has a cold, wet, and rainy climate quite different from that of our Brazilian city).

We were still trying to adapt. Still trying to understand enough of the language to shop for groceries or order at a restaurant. Still living without friends. Still unaware of where to buy the best bread, which supermarket was most convenient, which hospital to go to in an emergency. The girls were still getting used to their new school, and my husband was still figuring out the responsibilities of his new job. We still hadn't decided whether we would buy bicycles for the whole family or not, since Brussels is a flat city, but it rains a lot.

After all, we had only been there for two months.

Here, I make a note for the expatriate or immigrant woman, or anyone considering living abroad: only a woman who moves to another country with her family knows the sheer number of small things that turn into big things to do, think about, decide on, and learn. There are so many variables for the whole family—for the husband and the children. But for the woman, the ongoing to-do list is incredibly endless.

Then came the "lock…what?" announcement. It hit us as if it were the car and we the brick wall, right in the middle of all those small-big tasks. And there we were— unable to resolve anything, unable to buy anything because everything had shut down suddenly.

The only option for us was, once again, to face the moment with positivity, good energy, and a willingness to embrace whatever lessons this phase of family life would bring.

For an entire year, we stayed closed off in our little world.

The Inner Journey

Isolated completely from the outside world, I was forced to begin a journey of repairing my internal world. A journey of opening myself up to this new phase of personal growth. It became a journey to rediscover Camila as an individual—a unique, solitary person with her own interests, essence, talents, and life purpose. To step away, even briefly, from Camila the daughter, mother, wife, and HR executive. It took many highs and lows before I fully understood that starting over is not a weakness but rather the greatest act of self-love.

Navigating experiences was torturous—for example, needing technical support for something and not being able to communicate except through miming, intuition, or a translation app, or going to the supermarket and buying floor cleaner thinking it was laundry detergent because you don't speak the language.

Belgium is an incredibly beautiful country. One of the smallest in Europe, it borders the Netherlands, Germany, Luxembourg, and France, and it has three official languages—Flemish, a variant of Dutch; French; and German—along with various regional dialects. So you can imagine how confusing communication can be in that country.

But the most challenging experience wasn't the language or adapting to the new environment. The greatest challenge for me was adapting to becoming a new version of Camila—one who no longer worked for an organization, who no longer faced career challenges, who no longer interacted with colleagues (or, really, with anyone).

Deep down, I felt I couldn't exist solely to serve my family when my life's mission had always been to serve and help others. I can say that my journey of self-discovery began at that moment. I knew I needed to reconnect with my essence, but I didn't know how.

I knew I needed to embrace my personal change. To embrace it with my soul. To be kind without criticizing myself for not working intellectually or for not earning an income from my work.

I made the decision to leave my job, to put my long and successful career on hold—a career built with so much dedication and love. *I* decided to leave my country as a plus-one to my husband's expatriation. *I* made this decision; no one forced me.

I also decided, of my own accord and at my own risk, to create beautiful expectations for this change, starting with living in Europe. I found it glamorous, thrilling even, to move from Brazil, an emerging economy, to a developed nation with an advanced economy, high living standards, and a solid infrastructure. To one of the richest countries in the world. I was happy and enjoyed the opportunity I had been given to travel and live well. I just hadn't expected the pandemic.

But the pandemic was coming to an end, so yes, I could finally start living out my expectations. By the time the lockdown was lifted, we'd adjusted. Life in Brussels had taken shape. My daughters were thriving in school. We'd bought bikes and explored the city's parks and hidden playgrounds. I was practicing my French after immersing myself four hours a day during "lock...what?" New friends—mostly Brazilian, but also Belgian—had become like family.

The Call to Mexico

But there, in that room, at that moment, our destiny was determined once again when the call came.

My husband closed the door, asked me to sit, and said, "Mexico. We have a job offer in Mexico."

That's when the spit hit my face.

I felt the ground beneath me open up. My first question was, "Do we really have to go?" When I got no answer, the second was, "Can we make a list of pros and cons before we decide?"

He answered, "Sure, Cacá." That's what he's called me since we met.

He agreed, but deep down we both knew the answer. We already knew there would be more pros than cons. I just wanted to see it with my own eyes to make peace with it. But, really, deep down, I didn't want to see the pros.

Long story short, Mexico was our next step.

That night—sad, angry, exhausted, and hopeless—I cried myself to sleep. I didn't want to start over again. I didn't think I had the courage.

I should have gone to bed thoughtful. Perhaps grateful for my husband's career with so many opportunities and achievements, for our health, for the lives and growth of my daughters (in every sense), for the new cultural experiences that were yet to come.

But I didn't want to start over again. And, worse, I didn't think I had the courage to start over. At least…that day… that's what I thought. And I broke down.

That night, I was definitely no longer the Camila from a year and a half ago:

> *She spent her whole life thinking and executing.*
> *She did many things. Helped many people and*
> *companies. Was part of many challenging projects.*

51

Worked fifteen hours a day. Every day. For weeks, months, years. She realized many dreams. Achieved important positions. Was highly valued. Had money, bonuses, salary increases, many promotions. She was a powerhouse professionally.

And suddenly, without a recipe for success, her freedom and independence were frozen to build the happiness and wholeness of her family in another country. And her life changed completely. She no longer had the right to make her own choices.

The process of moving to Mexico completely shook me. My body and soul were devastated. I couldn't recognize myself in my lack of hope, optimism, ability to face things calmly, or in my lack of energy. Suffering from the autoimmune disease Hashimoto's thyroiditis, my body was hormonally imbalanced. I exhibited excessive fatigue, irritability, emotional unpredictability, sadness, and hopelessness.

I had already started my self-knowledge process in a more organized and intentional way months before the fateful news of our move to Mexico. I had also begun to study and connect with my spirituality through meditation and energy techniques, but nothing could pull me out of the hole. I had no willpower.

I didn't have the courage to face a country I didn't want to live in. I had always told my husband that we could live anywhere in the world...except Mexico. To me, Mexico meant drug cartels, heavy traffic, pollution, and danger. That's why it felt as if my husband had slapped me in the face.

Reinventing Myself

I spent three months—from the day the decision was made until the day of departure—focusing on the negative side of everything. I didn't even bother to properly research schools. The school my daughters would attend was chosen based on the number of Brazilians enrolled. I remember telling my husband, "Where do the children of the Brazilians working with you go to school? Then that's where they'll go if they're accepted." And that's where they went.

One night before the move, while getting lost in the streets of Brussels, I realized that I was more lost on the inside than I was on the outside. I had no control over anything. After reflecting on that, I decided to be kind to myself. I chose to go with the flow and let things unfold without overpreparing. After all, I knew from experience that, no matter how prepared you are or how many expectations you have beforehand, many things just don't work out the way you planned.

So I adopted the strategy of trusting the process in order to avoid losing control altogether. In that manner, lost within myself but determined not to control anything, we arrived in Mexico City. It was August 2021.

Today, I understand that starting over is about making space for new dreams, even when the weight of the past still burdens you. Mexico City, commonly known as CDMX, provided me with realized dreams and wonderful experiences. It's a shame I couldn't see that from the beginning.

My journey here has been filled with significant new beginnings. Beginnings that allowed me to build a story of self-discovery and personal transformation. Beginnings that led me to where I am today and helped me recognize my life's mission: to inspire souls to develop through self-knowledge and spirituality.

In Mexico City, I learned to stop and look within myself. It was because I moved to Mexico that I fell in love with numerology, got certified, and embarked on a course of development using this incredible tool of self-knowledge. Through it, I learned to look at myself differently, with more kindness, accepting my challenges, strengthening my abilities, and creating opportunities and solutions to resolve everything that needed to be resolved. I was able to reconnect with myself, with my essence, my talents, and my life's purpose. And through it, today, I allow myself to help women navigate their own transformations.

Looking back, I see that my two moves to different countries in such a short time forced me to realize how remarkable it is that life automatically pushes us into models imposed by society, religion, family, and work. These models often disregard what we truly want for ourselves. They block our talents, our truths, and our soul's essence.

I faced many challenges in leaving my previous life behind, but it was this path that allowed me to find new goals and passions. It was in the unknown and chaotic Mexico, while resisting the call, that I rediscovered my true essence.

The chaos of Mexico has its charms. My internal chaos had its own as well. Alternating between the chaos of this big city and my own internal chaos, I learned that chaos can be a gift. It can lead to action, new learning, new discoveries filled with surprises, beauty, and meaning.

Mexico surprised me. I found my true essence there. It is a country of true essence. Mexico is vibrant streets, warm people, and colorful culture; it is joyful and authentic. The mild climate is cold without being cold, hot without being overwhelming.

Through the streets of Polanco or the commercial center of Santa Fe, passing by the Zócalo and the Angel of Independence, the Saturday bazaar, or even inside my office with its view of the street, I was inspired to think that I didn't need to demand so much from myself or have all the answers to take the first step...or the next...toward a different Camila. A Camila with a different worldview. A Camila who reinvented not only herself but her career. A Camila who prioritized her own well-being, the value of her life, and her family's.

I learned to take risks, to put new ideas and projects into practice, even when I didn't feel 100 percent ready. I learned I could be authentic in my essence.

In Mexico, everyone can be authentic. Mexico is a country of connections within its multiculturalism. It teaches you to expand your perspectives and make yourself part of something greater.

Mexico enriched my life through new cultural interactions and new relationships. Here, my relationships have meaning; they are based on trust, mutual support, and family love, even from those who are not biological family. Here, I was able to test new paths, launch myself as a teacher and mentor for women going through transformations and seeking purpose and a balanced life. I reinvented myself and realized that life always offers new chances, as long as we have the courage to accept them.

Today, I share with the women who follow me, my students, and my friends the message that a woman's strength lies in her ability to reinvent herself, even when everything around her seems uncertain. Starting over in a strange place is a journey that teaches us that the true home is within us. And it is up to us—no one else—to cultivate that home.

Mexico taught me that home is not a physical place but a feeling within us. Our true sense of belonging and security comes from within. You can't seek external security or an external sense of belonging in any country. It's intrinsic.

Starting over is an act of self-care and hope. Life challenged me to leave the known behind so I could become what I am capable of being. A journey of change, when connected to the process of self-knowledge, emphasizes personal growth beyond the limits you once knew. Opportunities are always within our reach. We just need to look. But we need to be well enough to see.

My Hashimoto's disease is under control. With an intentional and consistent attitude, I have developed healthy habits for eating, exercising, and honing spiritual intelligence, and I am a Reiki master. Today, I run a community of incredible women focused on self-discovery, mental health, and well-being.

My journey has taught me that courage to start over is the greatest gift we can give ourselves. It allows us to grow, to thrive, and to find purpose even in chaos. And this is only possible because of what I have learned in Mexico. Because of my wonderful life in Mexico.

Studying neuroscience, I now know that our brain will always prefer the easiest path. But the easiest path is not always the best for us. In fact, I would venture to say that difficulty makes us stronger, and the challenges we overcome are responsible for our memorable moments. Happiness is totally connected with memorable moments of joy.

Leaving your comfort zone is the secret to a life of achievements and even more meaning. The new can be scary, but it's what pushes us forward. No matter how difficult, every new beginning offers an opportunity to create something extraordinary. We only need the courage to take that first step. And if it's scary, do it anyway.

The courage to begin again is the pathway to becoming who we are truly meant to be.

My hope for each person is that I have instilled in them passion, perseverance, resilience, and a relentless drive to succeed.

Manila, Mexico, and Me

Elizabeth Lloyd

There are a lot of similarities between Mexico and the Philippines. Both nations were part of the Spanish Empire. In 1521, Hernán Cortés conquered the Aztec Empire; in the same year, Ferdinand Magellan traveled to Asia and claimed the Philippine islands for the Spanish crown. Most Mexicans and Filipinos have mixed heritage, which explains the presence of Spanish words in Tagalog. This phonetic similarity is no coincidence but a reflection of the deeply intertwined histories of both nations.

Mexico and the Philippines are bound by a history of conquest and cultural transformation. Before Spanish rule, both thrived with distinct indigenous civilizations—Mexico's pyramids stand as testaments to its past, while the Philippines' rice terraces reflect a deep connection to the land. Then came the conquistadors, imposing Catholicism, and the reign of King Philip II, leaving both nations scarred by oppression. Strangely, both Mexicans and Filipinos seldom dwell on this painful legacy (especially the Philippines, as their country bears the name of the very king who orchestrated their suffering).

As Filipino historian Ambeth Ocampo stated: "The Philippines and Mexico are bound not just by history but by blood, language, and culture—two nations shaped by the same colonial experience yet charting their own destinies." This highlights the shared influences between the two countries due to Spanish colonization and the Manila-Acapulco Galleon Trade.

As I walked through the beautiful tree-lined streets of Polanco with its gorgeous colonial architecture in February 2018, I experienced an amazing sense of déjà vu. The tree-lined streets of Polanco are so comparable to the white Kalachuchi or plumeria obtusa trees that line the streets of Makati, Manila. It occurred to me that perhaps this feeling of familiarity was because my birthplace, the land of my maternal lineage, was in the Philippines. My grandmother, Esperanza Lazaro de Baxter, had moved to Manila from Barcelona in 1952 with her then ten-year-old daughter, Margarita (my mother), hoping for a new life after escaping the oppression of Franco's regime. My grandmother was my Bela. This moniker, Bela, was a result of my disabling childhood stutter. I could not pronounce my *A*'s, so *abuela* (grandmother in Spanish) became Bela.

Aside from this deep, sudden feeling of familiarity, I was drawn to Mexico City for a chance to start over personally and professionally. Having lived in San Francisco, California, for a long time, I was longing for something new—a new experience, a new adventure. Having been brought up in a very international household (a mother originally from Barcelona but moved to Manila at a very young age, and a father from Melbourne but lived in Hong Kong for most of his life), I was ready for a new challenge in a very cosmopolitan and fun city.

As a little girl, I always wanted to be involved in international business. It comes as no surprise then that I started my first company at the age of twenty-five, an online marketing company focused on international markets. I then went on to start another international online marketing company, co-headquartered in both Silicon Valley and London. How I loved all my business trips abroad, speaking at conferences in Sydney, Shanghai, and London. Meeting so many interesting people from different countries and cultures. That is what always kept me motivated, the chance to make so many different business contacts in different countries, most of whom ended up being friends, even to this day.

After I left my second company, I had no idea what to do. Both my head and feet were itchy, craving a new challenge, a new experience. Like a racecar driver who is addicted to the speed of going from zero to sixty, I love creating; starting something from zero pumps the adrenaline through my veins. In 2017, I attended a fintech conference in San Francisco, Lendit, searching for an international perspective. It was then that I attended a panel on online lending in Latin America, primarily Mexico, and a light bulb came on in my head. Why not take my business model from Silicon Valley/London to Mexico?

PING.

The light bulb literally became a spotlight. That evening, as I sat at my kitchen table in San Francisco, I researched endlessly to learn about possible competitors, market opportunities, and potential clients:

> Competition: *Nada*/Nothing
> Market Opportunity: Seemed Promising but Unknown
> Potential Clients: Some

With perseverance, patience, and a prayer, I knew that I could recreate the success of my second company in Mexico. No analysis paralysis, no business plan, no forecasting—nothing they teach you in business school about entrepreneurship. Just a go-getter attitude that I have had since childhood and a serious desire to prove myself again on a personal and professional level (coupled, as you may have surmised, with an extreme ADHD diagnosis).

The next day, I went to my mother's house on Arguello Boulevard in San Francisco; I told her about my new business idea and how I needed a new company name. My mother, a native Spanish and Tagalog speaker, enthusiastically got out her Spanish dictionary, closed her eyes, opened to a random page, and pointed to the word *ojo* (*eye*, in English; also used in Spanish to mean "keep an eye on," "pay attention to," or "be careful with"). My favorite number is seven, having been born in 1977, and my beloved grandmother's birthday, my Bela's birthday, was August 7. Thus, OJO7 was born. Domain bought through GoDaddy: check. LLC formed in Delaware and in California: check. I got started on the website, ordered business cards, and as my late father would always say in his deep Australian accent, "And we're off to the races."

It was fun. The endless stalking for potential clients on LinkedIn, the multiple redesigns of my consumer-facing brands, such as AmigoLoans.mx, until my bounce rate was minimal. The late-night searching for potential partners, sending cold emails to anyone who had a consumer finance site in Mexico. And everything just clicked. As John Quincy Adams said, "Patience and perseverance have a magical effect before which difficulties disappear, and obstacles vanish." This quote has guided me throughout my twenty-five-plus-year career.

Then it was time. February 2018. Time to visit Mexico City for my first batch of business meetings with potential clients and partners. Before that, the first and last time I had visited Mexico City was in December 2001. I was in route to Havana, Cuba, with my greatest love at the time (or so I thought at twenty-four years old). We stayed at La Casona in Zona Rosa, a beautiful colonial hacienda converted into a hotel, and walked around the Zocalo, admiring the beauty of its ruins, the last vestiges of the once-powerful Aztec Empire, now reduced to a shell, strategically placed right next to the colossality that is the cathedral designed by the Spanish but built by the Aztec slaves. What a juxtaposition. Love that word, *juxtaposition*—two things being seen or placed close together with contrasting effect. The best example of the meaning of this word is right there, in the heart of the Zocalo in Mexico City. Once the revered, feared, and respected cradle of the Aztec Empire, Tenochtitlán. Now reduced to shamans selling *palo santo* cleanses, vendors selling

Aztec-inspired trinkets made in China, and the pungent smell of *esquites* (delicious corn in a cup with a pinch of mayonnaise). The word *esquites* comes from the Nahuatl word *ízquitl,* which means "toasted corn." Highly recommended. As Carlos Fuentes, a renowned Mexican novelist wrote, "You graft a modern city onto a pre-Hispanic civilization, overlay it with 300 years of colonialism, and you have Mexico City."

We strolled past the Palacio de Bellas Artes, the cultural center in Mexico City where the repertoire includes ballets, exhibitions, performances. As we admired the art nouveau and neoclassical exterior, we noticed how comparable the architecture is to the Paris opera house, Ópera Garnier (and for the architectural buffs reading this, yes, I know that opera house has a neobaroque style). We ate the street food, its cilantro- and salsa-filled tacos with an abundance of limes. We drank tequila. We danced. We had fun in such an awe-inspiring city. Mexico City is a beautiful chaos— where ancient temples meet traffic jams, tacos are a way of life, and every street corner hums with history, music, and a little bit of magic.

That relationship ended, my heart broken into one thousand and one pieces. However, my love and affection for Mexico City didn't. Fast-forward seventeen years later, I arrived again at Benito Juarez International Airport. This time alone and armed with a deep conviction that I was going to build a successful online marketing company once again, but this time in Latin America. I was on a mission.

My meetings went well. I was feeling excited and hopeful that indeed OJO7 would succeed here. That trip was one of many, flying back and forth between San Francisco and Mexico City. The less than four-hour flight already seemed routine to me, part of my daily life. I was filled with excitement and uncertainty every time I landed at the airport, which was named after Benito Juárez, one of Mexico's most revered historical figures. He was the country's first indigenous presidents (of Zapotec origin), and he played a crucial role in shaping modern Mexico. Juárez is often associated with reform, modernization, and resistance against foreign intervention (notably against the French invasion and Emperor Maximilian).

As the months flew by and the business grew, it became more and more apparent that I needed to be in Mexico City on a full-time basis. I started hiring a local team. My first employee, Niza, was a result of an Uber ride from the airport to my Airbnb in Polanco.

Amazed at my Spanish fluency, "*¿Qué haces en la Ciudad de México?*" the driver asked. (Translation: "What are you doing in Mexico City?")

As a sidenote, I will always be so grateful to my grandmother and mother who raised me in a bilingual household. I didn't realize when I was younger what a blessing and a gift it would be to be fluent in Spanish. As George Bernard Shaw famously declared, "Youth is wasted on the young."

I explained to the driver that I was in Mexico City to start my new online marketing company, OJO7.

"*¿En línea como qué?*" he asked. (Translation: "Online, like what?")

I responded, "You know, marketing in Facebook, Google, everything online."

In the rearview mirror, I saw his eyes light up like a Christmas tree. *"Mi hija siempre está en Facebook."* (Translation: "My daughter is always on Facebook.")

As timing would have it, I was looking for a very junior person to attend to all our Facebook users, a customer service/community management role. *"Perfecto,"* I told him. *"Dame su WhatsApp y le marco."* (Translation: "Perfect. Give me her WhatsApp, and I will call her.")

OJO7's first-ever employee was the daughter of my Uber driver. Niza was her name. And because of Niza's friends, who also were Facebook addicts/junkies, my team started getting bigger and bigger. Much like Forrest Gump said, "Life is like a box of chocolates; you never know what you're going to get." My version: "Life is like an Uber ride; you never know who will be driving you." In my case, I got the original gangsters of OJO7. My first local team.

As the workdays got longer and the business prospered, I was finally at a point that I could enjoy Mexico and all it had to offer in terms of beaches, *Pueblos Mágicos*, cities. As an avid traveler (seventy countries), I really wanted to explore Mexico, the country. As Seneca wrote, "Travel and change of place impart new vigor to the mind." One of the first things I bought myself at a magazine stand in Avenida Reforma was a book on the *177 Pueblos Mágicos* located in each of the thirty-one Mexican states. The literal translation of *pueblo mágico* is "magical town," and indeed they are. To be recognized as a Pueblo Mágico, each town needs to have a rich cultural and historical heritage. Many Pueblos Mágicos have played an important role in Mexico's history or have a unique cultural tradition that sets them apart. They also must have vigorous preservation policies, ensuring a high standard of preservation and upkeep, and unique natural or architectural beauty. My goal was to visit one Pueblo Mágico every weekend. So away I went via bus, Uber, plane, or any other form of transport to get to these stunning gems. My favorites: San Cristobal de las Casas, San Miguel de Allende, Tequila, Todos Santos. Every now and then, I go back to that book, having earmarked each town's page, and my memories fill me with happiness that I got to experience such unique places. Sadly, some Pueblos Mágicos now are considered "dangerous" to visit due to cartel/narco activity. I will always cherish my solo Pueblo Mágico weekends during 2018 and 2019.

And here I am, exactly seven years later, in Mexico City. This year is a milestone, the seven-year anniversary of OJO7, my seven-year anniversary of living here. It is also the Year of the Snake in the Chinese Lunar New Year, for those born, like me, in 1977. And in the seven years I have been here, I have grown so much professionally, but more importantly, personally. It has been a beautiful experience filled with both positive and negative, as most things in life are. Overall, I have a new sense of resilience, self-confidence, and spiritual enlightenment. There are so many facets of Mexican culture and tradition that I respect and am so grateful for. One of them specifically is the esoteric side; they seem to recognize that each human being is made up of energy. As a result of this, I am more aware of the energy I have and the energy I want to have around me. When you think about it, emotions are energy in motion, e-motion. I love that.

And with this energy of resilience, of hope, of wanting a new beginning, I fondly think about the parallels not only between the Philippines and Mexico, but also between my grandmother and me, both independent women moving to a new land where they know no one and creating a beautiful life. (Sidenote: I did know one person in Mexico City, my dear friend Annie from boarding school, our friendship born when we were both thirteen-year-old girls at Santa Catalina School.) My grandmother and I are both pioneers. In the 1950s, she embarked on a long journey in a double-propeller plane to the Philippines from Spain; she had no idea how her life would evolve. Sixty-six years later, I moved to Mexico from California with only per-severance, patience, and a prayer, hoping it would all work out.

In Manila, my grandmother became an amazing accom-plished woman. She won the Premio Zobel, the Filipino version of the Nobel Prize, for her literature. I can't believe my own grandmother, born in 1919, has her own Wiki-pedia page due to all her accomplishments (for those of you interested: https://es.wikipedia.org/wiki/Esperanza_L%C3%A1zaro). Bela was a well-recognized figure in the art and literary circles; not only did her writing garner attention, but so did her copper artwork (one can be found in the halls of the Philippine Consulate General in San Francisco).

Similar to my grandmother, I too have been recognized here in Mexico for my professional accomplishments and my entrepreneurial journey. I am proud of the company I created here. I am proud of my team and the fact that most of them have been with me since 2018. My goal for each one of them is that they embark on their own entrepreneurial journey after their time at OJO7. I want all of them to have their own companies, their own paths. My hope for each person is that I have instilled in them passion, perseverance, resilience, and a relentless drive to succeed. That is probably the most important way I can pay it forward to Mexico, México Lindo, the country I love. If I can accomplish that, then I have accomplished what I was meant to. As my audio mentor, Jim Rohn, always says in every podcast, "Leaders create leaders."

And as for the next seven years, as Woody Allen famously said, "If you want to make God laugh, have a plan." I am a firm believer in this. Much like my grandmother when she moved to Manila, I too didn't know what to expect when I first moved to Mexico. Luckily, for both of us, it worked out. With hope, resilience, and gratitude, everything is possible. Onwards and upwards. *¡Vamos por más!*

Through every transition,
I have learned to embrace
change rather than fear it.
I've learned that flexibility,
resilience, and trust in the
journey can open doors
I never imagined.

A Fresh Start: Reinventing Myself in Mexico

Maria Paula Prieto

The Call for Change

My idea of a "perfect life" in Colombia was formed at eighteen, living independently, going to college, and building my future. I was studying government and international affairs, a path I felt passionate about. My days were filled with school, hanging out with friends, and enjoying the rhythm of life I had built for myself. But when my mom made the decision to move to the United States in search of better opportunities, everything changed. At eighteen, I was left to make a tough choice: stay in Colombia or follow my family. I chose to go, though the transition was far from easy.

The first few months were a whirlwind of uncertainty. I had to learn a new language, adapt to a culture that was so different from my own, and grapple with the feeling of being uprooted from everything I knew. The overwhelming emotions of sadness and fear were my frequent companions. I struggled with my friends being so far away; the busy, impersonal lifestyle; and the isolation I felt in a country that never quite felt like home.

I focused on pushing through, telling myself that success would come if I kept moving forward. I enrolled in English classes, worked full-time to avoid accumulating debt, and eventually graduated from college. Though my professional life was taking shape in the US, I never fully felt as if I belonged. I worked in education, developed a career in community engagement, and found great fulfillment in serving others. Still, there was always something missing—a deeper sense of home, connection, and fulfillment.

Arrival in Mexico: A New Beginning

In 2018, my husband's career presented an opportunity to relocate outside the US. Mexico was one of the options, and we began imagining a new life there. Though the transition took time to finalize, once it became certain, I felt an excitement that outweighed my worries.

This move was different from my first relocation. I was no longer a young woman following my parents; I was now the emotional head of my household. My daughters would be influenced by my attitude toward the move. While I didn't have to grapple with a language barrier this time, I still faced myriad uncertainties: leaving my job, giving up financial independence, finding schools for my kids, and establishing a new social circle.

Arriving in Mexico, my first priority was ensuring my daughters were settled and comfortable. I found a school for them and focused on helping them adjust. Once they were more stable, I began searching for ways to make my own transition smoother. I explored clubs to join, skills to develop, and work opportunities to consider. In these early months, I quickly noticed how family gatherings, socializing, and enjoying the local culture were big parts of life in Mexico. I reveled in exploring the food, the vibrant markets, and the walkable neighborhoods. The people were warm and welcoming, and I knew this would be a great place to start anew.

My daughters, however, were less enthusiastic. At the time, they were fourteen and seven, and the move felt like a huge sacrifice for them—leaving behind their friends, school, and extended family. Despite their resistance, I worked hard to highlight the positives about Mexico. "Everything in Mexico is perfect for Mom" became a family joke, but in my heart, I knew this new chapter was full of possibilities. And for the first time, I had the chance to immerse my daughters in the Spanish language and culture—something I'd always dreamed of but couldn't achieve in the US.

The Challenges of Change

The first few months in Mexico were focused on settling my daughters. Finding a school where they felt safe and supported was my top priority. Once they were stable, I began to look for ways to occupy my own time.

Leaving my job in the US was a significant shift for me. I had built a career in community engagement, working with underserved populations and developing programs that made a real difference. But now, I had to rediscover who I was outside of that role. Being a stay-at-home mom for the first time was difficult, and I found myself grappling with feelings of uncertainty.

An opportunity arose to work for an education start-up as a partnerships manager, promoting college-coaching services. It was a role I enjoyed for over two years, not only professionally but personally—it helped me guide my own daughter through the college-applications process. At the same time, I was involved in volunteer work with an international women's club and the parent organization at my daughters' school.

During this time of reflection, an old dream—one I had long buried—resurfaced. When I was in high school, I had wanted to pursue a career in the sports industry, specifically as a sports broadcaster. But in 1995, in Colombia, such a dream was unthinkable, especially for a young woman. I had put it aside, believing it would never be a realistic career path. However, living in Mexico gave me the freedom and the opportunity to finally revisit that dream.

Finding Your Footing: A New Path Forward

The job at the start-up revealed a hidden talent for event management that I hadn't recognized in myself. I was responsible for organizing numerous events, from small meetings to large conferences, and that experience brought me great satisfaction. As I got more involved at my daughters' school, I was elected PTA president, which required that I organize the school's biggest fundraiser.

Leading that project helped me hone new skills and taught me the power of collaboration. The school was going through a transitional period, and many parents were frustrated. I was fortunate to work with all the stakeholders to build a closer, more supportive community. This experience proved that leadership skills, once developed, can be applied in any situation. I learned that I could rally people around a common cause and that the lessons I had learned throughout my career could be transferred into any context.

Building a Meaningful Life

By the time I had completed my master's degree in sports broadcasting, I had a deep sense of satisfaction—but I also knew that a degree alone wouldn't open doors. I needed experience. I needed credibility. I had spent years building a reputation in community engagement and education, but now I was essentially starting from scratch in an entirely new industry.

It was daunting. I was in my forties, competing with bright, young professionals fresh out of college, all of them eager and hungry to prove themselves. Many of them had already spent years interning, networking, and getting their foot in the door while I was still trying to figure out where to begin. There were moments when self-doubt crept in. Was I being unrealistic? Was I setting myself up for failure?

But then I reminded myself why I was doing this. I had spent years telling my daughters to never settle, to go after what they truly wanted, to take risks and trust in themselves. How could I stand by those words if I wasn't willing to do the same? If I was going to teach them that dreams were worth chasing, then I had to be willing to chase my own—no matter how unconventional or difficult the path might be.

I started looking for internships, networking at every possible opportunity, and learning as much as I could about the industry. But rejection became an inevitable part of the process. I applied for roles I knew I was qualified for, only to receive polite rejection emails or, worse, no response at all. The uncertainty of not knowing if I'd ever get my foot in the door was frustrating, but I knew that if I wanted this badly enough, I had to keep going.

One day, while scrolling through job postings, I came across an opportunity to intern at a radio station covering the women's soccer league. It wasn't a high-paying job. It wasn't a leadership role. It wasn't even a guaranteed long-term position. But it was exactly the kind of opportunity I had been waiting for. I applied immediately, and after an interview process filled with nerves and excitement, I got the internship. I was officially stepping into the sports industry.

I'll never forget the first time I walked into Estadio Azteca with a press pass in hand. I had been there before, but always as a spectator, sitting in the stands, watching the game from afar. Now, I was on the other side, walking through the halls as part of the media, preparing to cover the match. I felt an overwhelming mix of emotions— excitement, disbelief, pride. I was standing in the same press rooms I had seen on TV for years. I was part of something I had only ever dreamed about. I remember standing there, watching the players warm up, feeling the energy of the stadium, and thinking, *This is it. I made it here.*

The work itself was exhilarating. I wasn't just reporting on games; I was telling stories, highlighting the journey of athletes, especially women in sports. Women's soccer, in particular, had always been underrepresented, and I was passionate about bringing more visibility to these incredible athletes who worked just as hard—if not harder—than their male counterparts, but received only a fraction of the recognition. Beyond covering the matches, I started creating content, writing articles, and partici- pating in discussions that mattered to the sports world. Every interview, every report, every game I covered rein- forced that I was exactly where I was meant to be.

But it wasn't just about the work—it was about the journey that had led me here. I realized that every step I had taken—the years of community engagement, the leadership roles, the event planning, the challenges of relo- cation—had prepared me for this. I wasn't starting from scratch. I was bringing a wealth of experience, perspective, and skills that set me apart.

That realization changed everything. I stopped seeing myself as someone "late" to the industry. Instead, I saw myself as someone with a unique story to tell, someone who had the courage to reinvent herself, someone who could use her voice to elevate the stories of others. And then, just as I was beginning to find my rhythm, life threw me another curveball.

After a year of building my place in the sports industry, my husband was told that we were moving back to Atlanta. At first, I was devastated. I had worked so hard to establish myself in Mexico. I had built connections, gained credibility, and finally started seeing the results of my efforts. Moving back felt as if I was starting over yet again. Would I have to rebuild everything from the ground up? Would I lose all the momentum I had gained?

But then something clicked. I realized that, this time, I wasn't the same person who had arrived in Mexico years ago, unsure of what the future held. I had already proven to myself that I could navigate change, that I could start over, and that I could succeed no matter where I was. I had developed skills that were transferable, had built relationships that extended beyond borders, and—most importantly—had gained the confidence to know that my career in sports wasn't tied to one location.

The industry might be different in Atlanta, but my experience, my knowledge, and my passion were still mine to carry with me. This wasn't the end of my journey. It was just another chapter. And I was ready for it.

Reflection: Growth and Gratitude

Looking back, I see how every step of my journey prepared me for this moment. My time in community engagement taught me how to connect with people, navigate unfamiliar systems, and build strong, supportive communities. My work in education instilled a commitment to continuous learning. And my relocations—first to the US and then to Mexico—taught me resilience and adaptability.

Pursuing a career change in my forties, especially in a competitive and youth-driven industry, was daunting. But it reminded me that it's never too late to chase a dream. I've grown not only professionally but personally; I've learned to embrace uncertainty and trust in my ability to reinvent myself.

Of course, I had my doubts. I wasn't sure if it was wise to change careers at an age where so many opportunities might close down due to a new wave of younger professionals. But I kept going, motivated by the desire to show my daughters that they should never settle for anything less than their dreams.

The path wasn't easy. I had to face many fears, including starting over in a new industry with little experience. But I learned that the abilities and qualities I had developed over the years could transfer anywhere. Mexico taught me the importance of being open to receiving help, a lesson I had struggled with for years. And I learned that no matter where life takes you, the skills you've built are always valuable, and they stay with you.

Closing: A Hopeful Note

Today, as I continue to build my career in sports broadcasting, I am filled with gratitude—for the challenges that shaped me, the courage to start over, and the opportunities I found in Mexico. My journey is proof that reinvention is always possible, no matter your age or circumstances.

Every struggle, every uncertainty, and every moment of doubt led me to this place where I am finally doing what I love.

Through every transition, I have learned to embrace change rather than fear it. I've learned that flexibility, resilience, and trust in the journey can open doors I never imagined. I've come to realize that the abilities and qualities I have developed throughout my life are transferable—no matter the location, industry, or phase of life. The lessons of community engagement, leadership, and perseverance transcend boundaries, and I carry them with me into every new chapter.

If there's one message I want to leave behind, it's this: dreams don't expire. They might shift, evolve, or take longer to manifest, but they are always within reach for those willing to chase them. Believe in yourself, embrace the unknown, and trust that the best chapters of your life may still be ahead.

The people I've met along the way, many of whom have come and gone, have shown me the complexities of change.

New City, New Me: Finding Home Again

Patricia Pulido

Isn't it reassuring when children quickly adapt to a new school, giving parents the much-needed peace of mind that comes with a new beginning?

We arrived in Mexico City just days before school started; the excitement of a new beginning was mixed with the weight of uncertainty. My ten-year-old son seemed ready to embrace the adventure, while my eight-year-old daughter carried with her the sadness of leaving Brazil. It was evident in the way she spoke longingly of the friends she had left behind. As a mother, I felt caught between their emotions and my own anxieties about what lay ahead. The challenge of adapting to a new school, a new city, and an entirely different rhythm of life felt overwhelming at times.

When the first day of school arrived, it felt like the true test of our new life. My husband and I decided on the "rip off the Band-Aid" approach: We would drop the kids off at the bus stop, snap a quick photo with the First Day of School sign, kiss them goodbye, and hope for the best. I kept telling myself that the quicker the goodbye, the easier it would be for everyone.

It felt bittersweet to let go of our family tradition of taking a First Day of School photo in the front yard of our house, as we had always done in the past. Now, living in an apartment building for the first time, we had to adapt the tradition to our new surroundings. The photo we took in the dim morning light of our building's entryway became a quiet emblem of the subtle changes that lay ahead.

It was the first time I wouldn't be driving my children to school. I threw on, over my pajamas, the first pair of sweats I could find, and we stood together at what we assumed was the designated bus stop. Moments later, we watched in disbelief as the bus zipped past us on the opposite side of the avenue. In an instant, panic set in. With no time to figure out what went wrong, we jumped into the car, and for the very first time, I drove them to school by myself.

That day was full of firsts—not just for my kids, but for me, too. It was the first time we skipped our cherished front-yard photo. The first time we waited at a school bus stop and the first time I found myself facing the chaos of Mexico City traffic. The first time I felt so uncertain of what was to come.

Driving on the *Segundo Piso*, the elevated highway that looms over the city, was an adventure in itself. My heart raced as I merged into the relentless flow of cars. After years of calm and predictable small-city living, this was a sharp and sudden initiation into the pulse of a metropolis—an adventure I hadn't quite prepared for.

Entering the big school felt vastly different from the more intimate one they had attended in Brasília. Gone was the guard who greeted each child by name with a warm smile and a high five. In Mexico City, everything felt bigger, faster, and less personal.

As I stepped into the school's courtyard, the sight of the classic British school uniforms—stiff blazers, neatly tied ties, pleated skirts, and polished black-leather shoes—immediately transported me to my own childhood. Memories of my British school days, marked by strict rules and rigid expectations, came rushing back, stirring both nostalgia and unease about this new chapter. Standing in the middle of the bustling courtyard, overwhelmed by the commotion of the first day, I decided to ask some of the questions that had slipped my mind earlier.

Amid the chaos, I noticed a woman frantically gesturing, attempting to guide the confused crowd of parents and students. Assuming she was a coordinator, I approached her, hoping for some direction. "Excuse me…" I began, my voice hesitant.

She turned to me with a cold stare and in a clipped British accent snapped, "I don't have time for this right now." Her words hit me like a sudden slap, leaving me rooted in place, almost in tears from the sting of her response.

I couldn't believe it—I was the one falling apart, not my kids. I walked away feeling disappointed and unwelcome, the weight of her reaction lingering long after. With no one to share my frustrations, apart from my ever-supportive husband, the moment felt even heavier. I knew I needed comfort, but I also realized that some things would be different this time. I couldn't let myself fall into the trap of constant comparisons.

Despite my own uncertainties, I found comfort in watching my children adapt in their own ways. In those first weeks of school, my daughter proudly introduced herself as Brazilian to her peers and teachers. I didn't have the heart to correct her. It felt like a small gift—a way for her to anchor herself in something familiar amidst so much newness. In a community filled with international students, this simple act of self-identification reassured me that my third-culture kids, who don't see home as a single place, would find common ground with others navigating the same transient reality. I was especially grateful that eventually I was added to the Brazilian moms' chat group, even though they knew I was a Colombian who spoke fluent Portuguese. These small connections were truly priceless, and being part of a community felt like such a blessing—especially at a time when I still felt unsure of how my life would unfold as I searched for stability in the midst of so much change.

As the weeks turned into months, our life in Mexico began to take shape. Slowly but surely, I started to feel as if I belonged and was adapting to this new life. Yet, as

I reflect on the expat journey, I realize that the real challenge begins long before you feel settled—it starts the moment you tell your kids, "We're about to begin a new adventure!" That's when reality truly sinks in.

But when is the right time to share this news with your current tribe? That's a question that weighs heavily on the minds of many expats—a shared challenge of this nomadic lifestyle. It's usually asked while one foot is firmly planted in the present, and the other is stepping forward into the next chapter. This moment becomes a dividing line, marking the transition between the now and what lies ahead.

Will friends treat you differently once they know you're moving on? Perhaps. They may hesitate to invest time in a present friendship that's destined to become long-distance.

These questions lingered in the back of my mind even as I felt the thrill of receiving the news—"Next post: Mexico!" We had been so happy in Brasília, but the thought of moving to Mexico City felt as if it was a step up. It filled us with the courage to embrace the unknown and accept the offer with open arms.

The idea of returning to life in a bustling city was invigorating, stirring memories of my move to New York City more than two decades before—a pivotal time that taught me the art of reinvention. Each relocation brings more than just a change in scenery; it carries the promise of a fresh start, an opportunity to rediscover and redefine myself as "a new me in a new city." I've walked this path before—transforming from a business-major student in Bogotá to a fashion designer in New York City, then to a stay-at-home mom in Managua and Washington, DC, and even later to a family and birth photographer in Brasília. Every chapter has been a testament to adaptability, teaching me invaluable lessons about change. Yet, no matter how familiar the process, every move brings its own set of questions and uncertainties—reminders that growth is often accompanied by both excitement and doubt.

These uncertainties are frequently overlooked by others. I often hear people say, "It must be easy for you to pack up and move—you've done it so many times!" But is it really that simple? With each move, I find myself wondering, *Will I meet incredible friends like the ones I'm leaving behind? Will I still have my beloved karaoke nights? Will I find clients who truly appreciate the storytelling approach to photography? Will I discover a ceramics studio I enjoy as much as my current one? Will there be a gym that offers fun classes conveniently located near my new home?* These questions reflect the delicate balancing act of moving—managing the excitement of what's ahead with the nostalgia of what you're leaving behind.

It's a challenging process that requires embracing both emotions. However, over the years, I've come to understand that I lean toward optimism in these situations. I prefer to hit the ground running and not dwell too long on the challenges of adjusting to change. Instead, I channel my energy into building a sense of belonging wherever I go—focusing on new opportunities, connections, and experiences that make each move feel as if it is a fresh chapter waiting to be written.

This mindset has shaped how I approach each relocation. As an extrovert, finding my tribe has always been a top priority. Before moving to Mexico City, I did just as I had done in Brasília. I registered online for the International Women's Club before we even arrived; later I found the Association of Diplomatic Spouses. Both are remarkable organizations with decades of history; they offer incredible social support while actively fundraising for charities. Joining them gave me an instant sense of purpose and familiarity, which steadied me through the challenges of the transition.

Still, making new friends in a new city is not without its challenges. A friend once told me that building friendships is akin to playing the dating game, and that analogy has stayed with me ever since. It's all about finding the right connection—if you make it past the third time you hang out, it's a promising sign. If not, it's game over.

That perspective became even more relevant when we moved to Mexico City, where forming an extended family of friends to share this temporary journey felt essential. Over time, I've realized that it's not the location that matters most—it's the people you connect with. While each city brings its own unique experiences, it's those relationships that truly shape the way you live and thrive in a new place.

As I settled into our new life, my extroverted nature took over. Building connections has always been my anchor during transitions. My wonderful husband is always amused by how many people we randomly bump into on a daily basis. "Do you know everyone in this city already?" he jokes with a proud smile on his face.

The truth is, I thrive on building different circles of friends—the locals, the Latinos, the crafty ladies, the parents we can hang out with alongside the kids, my gym buddies, old college friends we've reconnected with, the Scout families, my fellow street photographers, etc. Each group brings something unique to our lives, creating a mosaic of relationships that has enriched our experience in Mexico.

Friends often describe me as a walking source of information, a know-it-all in the best way. I've come to realize that I genuinely enjoy searching for new plans and places, then offering tips or advice when friends—or even strangers—need it. I love discovering new spots, whether it's a new pop-up vintage clothing shop, an art exhibit, a great *trajinera* tour in Xochimilco, the handyman who will hang your frames, or the perfect guide who will tell you all about Teotihuacan pyramids. I spend hours browsing travel blogs, local forums, and group chats, piecing together recommendations to share with others. Staying in the loop about the best spots and resources has become my personal hobby. It's a way for me to share what I love and help others settle into their new lives.

Staying connected to the city and its resources gave me a sense of control and accomplishment, especially during those early months of adjusting to life in Mexico. I like to think I've conquered a move the moment the last cardboard box is unpacked. It took about six months to feel at home, and just as I started to fully embrace our new city, the pandemic hit. The vibrant lifestyle we'd been easing into came to a screeching halt. Mexico's relaxed approach to COVID-19 contrasted with the uncertainty of those early days. Slowly, the unease shifted to a new challenge— adapting to a life confined to our apartment. It became a mix of emotions: isolation paired with the unexpected gift of uninterrupted time spent as a family.

We found many ways to cherish our time together and Chapultepec Park became our refuge. Its vast greenery offered a sense of normalcy amidst the chaos, giving us a place to play, walk, and simply be with one another. Those moments of quiet simplicity helped us navigate the isolation and reminded us to focus on what truly mattered.

As the world began to reopen, so did my passion for street photography. I've always enjoyed the solitude of walking and observing people, which is one of the reasons I've been passionate about street photography for over a decade. There's something magical about wandering through the city with my camera, capturing its rhythms and intricacies.

Many of my vacation clients request sessions at Zócalo, and I never tire of the journey to get there. Taking the Metrobus along Reforma, riding on the top of the public double-decker bus, I watch the city unfold in layers through those windows.

The Zócalo itself never fails to captivate me. One of the largest city squares in the world, it is a swirling mix of colonial-era architecture, bustling vendors, and locals going about their day. I love capturing the busyness of the city while documenting families as they explore the streets.

After a photo session, I take time to lose myself in its surrounding streets, soaking in the energy and charm of downtown and sometimes adding a museum visit along the way. The markets are always a highlight for me—a sensory explosion of colors, scents, and sounds. Narrow sidewalks overflow with stalls as vendors call out in rhythmic chants, adding to the lively atmosphere. The smoky aroma of improvised grills sizzling with tortillas mingles with fragrant spices, creating an irresistible blend of scents that lingers in the air and forms the sensual background for a vibrant visual feast of colors and textures.

It's fascinating to see such an eclectic mix of offerings packed into a single block. Wandering through this maze of stalls, every stop brings a new discovery. I've filled my bag with Christmas piñatas, Day of the Dead accessories, colorful *milagrito* hearts as the perfect local souvenir, quirky board games for my kids, party supplies, fabrics, and threads to add to my stash. You name it—it's there!

Every trip to these markets feels as if it is a treasure hunt brimming with surprises and sentimental finds that enrich my everyday life in this vibrant city. I know I'll miss this unique experience when our time here inevitably comes to an end. Margaritas and tacos will never taste the same outside of Mexico—this country has forever spoiled me with its incredible food and cultural richness.

As the years pass—nearly six now—I've come to understand another layer of this nomadic journey. The people I've met along the way, many of whom have come and gone, have shown me the complexities of change. Watching close friends struggle to adjust to their new lives after leaving Mexico has been especially eye-opening. They often describe it as homesickness, but it's clear that what they truly miss isn't just a physical place—it's the lifestyle and the connections they left behind in a vibrant and unforgettable city.

This is why I believe so deeply in the power of photos and the importance of preserving memories. Life's fleeting moments—both joyful and challenging—weave the fabric of our stories. While memories may fade over time, printed images have a unique way of capturing and protecting them, providing a tangible and lasting link to the experiences that have shaped us.

I was once asked, "If you had to choose between being a family photographer or a photo organizer, what would you choose?" Without hesitation, my answer was to help safeguard personal photos and videos, which are testaments to the meaningful, raw visual stories of everyday life. Preserving and organizing the legacy is not just about looking back—it's about honoring the connections and experiences that define who we are, reminding us of where we've been, and helping us find gratitude for every step of the journey.

Reflecting back, I've come to understand that what matters most isn't the location itself, but the people you connect with and the community you become a part of. While every city offers its own unique experiences, the relationships you build truly shape how you live, grow, and thrive in a new place.

I've been incredibly lucky to find amazing communities wherever I've been, and for that, I am deeply grateful. These connections have shaped my path, and I will cherish them forever.

This journey has been one of transformation. Starting over isn't just about moving—it's about embracing uncertainty, finding beauty in the unfamiliar, and gathering the courage to grow through every misstep and victory.

Mexico City, with its chaos and charm, became the perfect setting for this change. It isn't just another temporary home—it has been a chapter that reminds me of the beauty of fresh beginnings and the power of reinvention.

We don't remember days; we remember moments.
—Cesare Pavese

This is where my story begins after feeling I had it all and needed nothing else, I lost everything and had to start over from the inside out.

The Journey to Self-Love

Maria Fernanda Rodriguez

I will start my story by telling you a bit about my past and about what my life has been like in the last year. Even though that is not what I want to focus on, it is an important step that gave way to what I will narrate in the rest of these pages.

When I was twenty-four, I met the man who would become my husband and the father of my children. As an anecdote, we used to say it was love at first sight; because the tenth time I saw him —we lived in different countries— I was walking towards the altar of a church on an idyllic and heavenly place in a mountaintop of Margarita Island in Venezuela.

Happily married, we lived together for almost eighteen years, had two children, lived in three different countries, and enjoyed countless moments together. Traveling and dining at the best restaurants were one of our favorite hobbies. At nights, we used to crack open a bottle of wine and laugh together at the most silly things.

When we were with our children, we enjoyed watching movies at home, even though I always fell asleep, after that, we discuss and analyze the movie. Our aim was always to set the best example for our children; we want them to be good human beings.

It never mattered where we lived; the doors to our home were always wide open to receive our friends and family who came to visit and spend time with us.

We had it all; we enjoyed every day of our lives in Mexico City. That's the way we were until our story came to an abrupt, unexpected end.

We had just come back from a trip —only he and I— when upon awakening the next day, I was hit headfirst with a reality I could have never imagined. I remember feeling as if a hole had opened beneath my feet; I literally fainted.

This is where my story begins—after feeling I had it all and needed nothing else, I lost everything and had to start over from the inside out. Since that morning, and every day that followed, my head had been filled with a thousand of questions, doubts, and uncertainty.

When it happened, my heart flooded with profound pain, and I felt my very soul detach from my body for a few seconds. The impact was so forceful that its effect was inversely proportional, the disappointment and heartbreak were so great that something inside me just as powerful was awakened.

Love changes just as much as
the people who support it.

—Nipur Bhasin

Inside me, a determined, strong woman awoke, a woman I had never seen before, a woman with a strength that pushed me to search and do whatever it took to recover and overcome. I could have stayed and fought to mend that which broke again, but there are things that, after breaking so much, become irreparable, and this was a sign from the universe letting me know I had to do things different from before. From that moment on, I became a brave, mature adult woman: I broke the cycle and left to prevent further injury and pain.

Despite everything that was going on, I decided to head down a path of self-love awareness. I realized that nothing is too big for me, that I could move forward with my two kids even if the country I was in was not my own. I decided to stay in Mexico because, obviously, going back to my home country, Venezuela, was out of the question. After making these first decisions, I started on the road to healing my heart and my soul without knowing what the final destination would be.

Even if it sounds cliché, I firmly believe in the saying "Everything happens for a reason." And what happened to me was meant to help me find true love, a love pure and authentic, a love bigger than any other, the self-love, that is my life's engine. I have recently learned that more important than knowing the final destination, more important than actually reaching it, is enjoying the journey. So, I have decided to do just that—take each step with enthusiasm and the energy to keep going, keep discovering life, keep living.

Was I scared? Very. But the road has taught me to overcome fear.

I know what happened was meant to happen in order to prepare me for something new, and that is how my self-love and self-discovery journey begins. In the darkest, saddest moment of my life, I decided to embark on an internal journey that turned out to be the magical first step toward self-discovery. Even though I was shattered at the onset, pain transformed into peace when I learned to accept the things that I could not change. Since then, I have decided to let go of what is already gone, what is no longer a part of me.

During my journey, I had a special experience with a Buddhist monk who taught me that pain is inevitable, that when we do not resist it, the pain becomes less intense, less lasting. So, I decided to embrace and live my pain and learned that eventually pain becomes transitory. I learned I cannot control my emotions, but I can control what I do when they wrest control of me, and that changed everything.

I recognized how important is to live with no attachments. Mental and physical attachments control and limit you, as they come at the expense of our freedom; they create an emotional dependency that does not allow for happiness.

I understood that my happiness is in my hands; it is my decision. So, I made happiness my life's goal—I vowed to be happy in spite of the circumstances, to live with no attachments, to be grateful for the privilege that surrounds me, for the experiences lived, and for love received that expands inside of me.

As my search progressed, I met a unique and special being who guided me through a trip towards self-love. I discovered that it is more than just a term; it is a deep process of rebuilding that I was able to discover in a magical way. Self-love starts as the tiniest of dots in the center of a circle. Then:

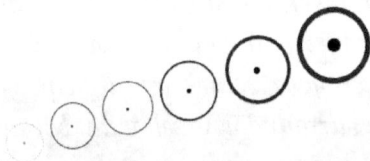

When we are born, we are an itty-bitty, tiny dot in the universe, and that dot receives and perceives different things from the outside (education, family context, religion, etc.), and as time goes by and with lived experiences, it evolves, grows, matures. It starts forming a character and a personality, it defines its preferences and values, and so it forms what I call a "wall" that shapes its life.

In the beginning, this "wall" that surrounds the dot is so frail that it can break; it can be easily infiltrated, though, in time, it grows stronger, and its base more solid.

It happens, as well, that the distance between the dot (you) and the "wall" broadens, even though it can also decrease. As with everything else in life, with time, this "wall" changes. It can grow stronger or weaker, and it can even completely disappear; the space it limits can decrease or widen.

That space between the dot and the "wall" starts filling with love—the love it gives and the love it receives, for love is a cyclical force that goes round the space and expands. It is a spiral with a multiplying effect.

This "wall," which can be seen as a companion and a caretaker, is your limit. Your limit molds you, your life, your conduct, your behavior, your self-respect, your values, and it helps you choose what you surround yourself with. Meaning, what you let in and what you reject. It is like a security gate: it defines what lets in, and what keeps out.

Here lies the importance of learning how to let go of what does not go with you, because, when this happens, you are opening a space to fill you with the things that are actually of benefit to you.

This spiraling magnetic force forever in motion between the dot and the wall is your self-love, which allows you to live at peace and find happiness, to enjoy life with no strings attached. It gives you the tools to face life.

This is why, as we grow older, evolve, and dedicate time to our personal development, self-love helps us strengthen that wall, and at the same time, we develop an intuition, a sixth sense, to identify any harmful object trying to cross that wall and destroy what we've built inside.

Self-love is an internal space that you create and strengthen with time, a space sacred to you, a space where you can decide what to let in or what to release. As your wall grows stronger and you learn to let in only what is good for you, you will have a whole, happy life. In that moment, in that state of self-awareness, it is easier to make decisions without any overthinking or uncertainty. When you make the right decisions in the right moment, you will be surprised at what the universe has in store for you. With love, the universe will always give back more than the amount you've given away.

That is when you will realize that, even if you love a person dearly, if this person is breaking the love bond you have created with yourself—and if instead of feeling loved, you are feeling broken—it is time to accept reality and take action. Otherwise, if you let this situation persist, it will steal the space of your self-love, and your self-love will weaken and lose power.

Self-love is the most genuine, most pure expression of love. It is the love you carry inside for you. It is your engine, the inner compass that will guide you down the right path. It takes care of you and protects you from the outside world. It is the motivation that allows you to evolve and keep growing, the giving act for yourself that recirculates inside you and keeps on growing and increasing in frequency, embracing you more and more.

After this journey, I was left profoundly touched and cried all night, but this time my tears did not come from pain but from recognition of self-love. Thanks to this experience, I learned to see and live self-love from another perspective. Love is inside us; we just have to recognize it and start to feel it. After living through this, I reflect and tell myself, *My marriage is not over because of what happened, it is over because I decided to put my self-love first.*

Today, a year from that dark moment, I am here, writing these lines, and I feel like a more solid person, strong and ready to face any challenge in life because I had the chance to work on myself, to get better and stronger, to build a greater wall.

Since this experience, I have also reflected on the importance of talking to children about self-love and the ways to cultivate it by constructing their own wall and strengthening it as they grow.

Let us not take anything for granted. Even self-love needs to be cultivated, taken care. Let us keep learning to make our self-love grow. It has to be strong and big enough to sustain us through the times we cannot sustain ourselves. It will give you certainty, security, the assurance that you can overcome anything. It will make you realize nothing is too big; your love is bigger than your problem, and therefore nothing is impossible.

The increase in the frequency of the spiral of love happens as we give pure, sincere love to everything that surrounds us; it increases when we grab our happiness without hurting anyone, when we are thankful for everything that life has given us, even the smallest thing, because we do not take anything for granted.

I start my day by being thankful for it; for being able to step out of bed, hug my children, have a warm cup of coffee between my hands, see the colors of sunrise through the window, and feel a ray of sunshine hit my face. I am thankful for the smallest and the simplest things, things of no monetary value, because that is the greatest blessing. And so, the day goes on, and I thank it. Life itself is an act of constant gratefulness.

Today, I am thankful to life for putting me here. Even though I did imagine a different path for myself, life presented me with a detour, and I am sure it is because the detour will take me to the right path. I am discovering and living life to the fullest, aware of my self-love. I have learned that life has not taken anything away from me; instead, it has gifted me with it all.

Life is change, and everything is a cycle. I have learned that you cannot love someone else without loving yourself first. First, I have to love myself; only then will I recognize true love and refuse to accept anything less. Love must add and multiply, not subtract and divide you into a little pieces.

I am thankful for this journey of self-discovery and self-love. I am thankful for every person who has crossed my path and helped me walk it.

> To my friends who sustained me;
> To The Inside Traveler, for the journey towards my true self is the most important trip I have made;
> To Soul-Searching Trip, which took me to the edge and beyond my mental abilities and taught me to challenge and trust myself;
> To Nipur Bhasin, Buddhist monk, from whom I learned that true happiness is only achieved when you let go of all attachments;

To the doctors and therapists, who took care of and guided me along this path;

To Isaac, who guided me to see and feel self-love from another perspective;

To the universe, for gifting me my dream job; where I love what I do, and I am so happy and I feel fulfilled;

To my parents and my family, who accepted my decision without questioning or judging me, and who have been with me all along, if only from a distance;

To God, who never let go of my hand and instead held it hard;

Thank you all.

And thank you, Life, for giving me the opportunity to live a new life in this same life!

This home, this family,
this life we have built
is an extension of my
identity—something
I once viewed through a
very narrow lens.

Untethered

Sadia Salam

There comes a time in life when you experience big changes. They can come from within, or you may see them approaching as you brace yourself. You're either *being* it or *seeing* it.

My name is Sadia, and this is my story. The story of a new beginning that changed everything around me, and a lot within me.

I was born in India and spent most of my life in New Delhi. It is a country as vast as it is varied, home to thriving industries, rich cultures, many languages, and endless opportunities. However, "living abroad" is a dream that is packaged and sold to us in movies. So did the dream of moving abroad manifest within me? The answer is both yes and no. Yes, because it did seem surreal to have the option to travel afar and open doors to new possibilities. No, because I was aware of the realities of a middle-class life.

I'm the eldest daughter of two self-made individuals, both retired journalists. For the first ten years after finishing my studies, my focus was on improving the quality of life for my parents, my sister, and me. By my late twenties, I had grown into a senior marketing role and was helping my family own our first home. It's interesting how many significant silent achievements go unnoticed, but still shape us into who we become. I was fulfilled, and perhaps it was the best time for love to knock on the door. And so it did.

The first time I met Alexis, there was something strangely familiar about him, which was surprising, as we had nothing in common except being in the same place at that moment. But I somehow felt more of a connection with someone born and raised over 4,000 miles away in the Basque country, Spain, than with most people I had met here. It was one of the most interesting revelations of my life. We spent hours talking about his Basque roots, my childhood in Delhi, what we love doing, what we want out of life, and the values that matter to us. It did not take us long to realize that we were meant to be together.

We spent a beautiful time discovering each other's cultures. Both our families welcomed our love with open arms, which made our union even more joyful. By the end of 2019, at a quaint fort in Rajasthan, India, friends and family from both India and Spain gathered to celebrate our wedding. What had begun as friendship was blossoming into a lifetime of togetherness, and life had never felt more beautiful.

We began planning our honeymoon, but little did we know that global travel along with everything else in the world was about to come to a screeching halt. The pandemic arrived and brought with it chaos and uncertainty. While we were still learning to adapt to the new way of life dictated by these circumstances, my husband was offered a role in Mexico, a country I knew little about and had never in my dreams imagined moving to. I felt as if I did not have enough information to make a decision, but it had to be done.

There was a lot going through my mind at this time: family, career, language barrier, new beginnings, and, most importantly, my independence. I fully supported my husband, who is incredible at what he does and deserved the opportunity that was at our doorstep. I started doing research, and it turned into a fun project that kept me curious and fascinated by every new thing I discovered. It became clear that pop culture had done a disservice to a multifaceted country like Mexico, failing to highlight the incredible depth of its culture. The decision to move became easy thanks to the outcome of the research.

As we prepared for the move, we encountered a harsh reality—the gap in our passport privileges. What had once meant me applying for visas and us in separate airport queues was now going to mean *a year of living apart*.

Two thousand twenty-one was the longest year of my life. Alexis was living in Mexico while I had to wait for my visa to be approved. We were 8,700 miles and eleven and a half hours away from each other. We celebrated our second wedding anniversary over a video call. We were in lockdown, so I could not even distract myself by stepping outside.

Music and therapy were two important things that helped me get through. There is a Bollywood song that talks about how birds, rivers, gusts of winds do not have to care about borders, but we humans do. I always loved it, but during that period, it felt like a hug.

The year did finally end, and I booked a one-way flight to Mexico. The question was, how do you pack your entire life in a suitcase or two? But then, you're not really moving if nothing is being left behind. I just packed the things that reminded me of my loved ones and as many dresses as I could. It takes about thirty hours to reach Mexico from India. My flight was through London, and I stopped there for a few days to be with my sister Munira, who was studying in the UK at that time.

"I'm going to pick you up," my long-distance husband said to me as I was preparing to leave London.

"Obviously, Alexis!" I exclaimed. "Were you not going to pick me up from the airport when I'm coming to you, leaving my whole life behind?"

He replied, "Sadia, I'm coming to London to pick you up, and we'll travel together to Mexico."

I was surprised and, to be honest, floored. He somehow knew that I had envisioned us walking into the new city together. The next day, we landed in Mexico City.

The first morning in Mexico City, I decided to take a short walk. The jacaranda trees were in full bloom, and there couldn't have been a better time to start afresh here. An hour passed, and I realized I was still walking, completely blown away by Polanco, the most happening part of the city. As I continued, I came across Museo Soumaya; its striking architecture instantly drew me in. The next hour was no less than a magical odyssey of art and creativity.

And then it hit me: I was all alone, yet I was enjoying every moment of it. Back home, I never would have gone to a museum by myself. There was always someone to share the experience with. But here, in this new city, I felt completely at ease—alone, but not lonely. It was as if the city was telling me things about itself, while also revealing things about me.

The following week, I decided to explore more of the city and visited Ciudadela, the handcraft market. I was amazed by the incredible work of Mexican artisans, and it reminded me of Indian craftsmanship. Interestingly, both cultures share a passion for vibrancy. The next thing on the list was food. I am a vegetarian, and initially that felt like a challenge, but I soon discovered that there is a small but active vegetarian/vegan community here.

By week three, the woman who was never interested in walking was logging more than ten thousand steps a day. The woman who always styled herself in heels was now out and about in *sneakers and a dress*, which is also the name of my social media profile. I found myself immersed in Mexico's glorious past, which was sometimes chaotic, sometimes peaceful, but always rich, containing layers I couldn't yet fully understand, but was eager to. In a funny way, it felt like dating—the stage where you're eager to learn everything about someone, mentally noting their likes and dislikes, weighing the pros and cons, and trying to find common ground where a connection could grow. What I hadn't realized back then

113

was that the seed of a strong connection had already been sown.

The language barrier did initially curtail my ability to have conversations, and Google Translate became my most-used app. But I knew in my heart that the most respectful and exciting thing to do was learn the language of the country that my husband and I wished to call home. If you choose to immigrate, you should also choose to integrate. I went online and looked for Spanish-language resources. Most of them advertise themselves with click-bait—for example, "Be fluent in two months!" Well, that's not how it works.

Most of us in India grow up bilingual—in my case, trilingual. Taking the count to four, I started learning Spanish through podcasts and books, and soon switched to one-on-one lessons. The best way to learn a language is immersion. It opens a wide new world for you to explore and dive into. From Frida Kahlo to Carmen Boullosa, the strength and will of Mexican women inspired me to the core.

A few months down the line, Google Translate wasn't the most-used app anymore. There was a subtle sense of liberation in being able to communicate, even if it was at a basic level. What made this experience emotional was the kindness and understanding of the Mexican people, and their willingness to help someone struggling to communicate. No judgment, no pressure—everyone I met offered support by finishing my broken sentences, encouraging me, and reassuring me that I was doing well. It truly reflected the values of empathy, grace, and humility that are deeply ingrained in the people of Mexico. *Poco a poco,*

I kept improving, and I still am. After all, Spanish had come into my life before Mexico did.

As the dust settled, the excitement of taking the biggest life-changing step started turning into a question—*I'm here. Now what?* And then there were several mornings when I did not feel that great. In the words of Ijeoma Umebinyuo:

> *So, here you are*
> *too foreign for home*
> *too foreign for here.*
> *Never enough for both.*

Moving abroad strips you of something you never realized you relied on—the quiet, unseen comfort of sensory familiarity. At some point you begin to notice how much of your emotional equilibrium depended on the small, everyday details of life that you took for granted. There are certain experiences in life that make you feel things that language fails to capture. So I tried to capture it in a poem that's now very close to my heart:

> *Everything familiar is far, far away.*
> *It's not a visit; I'm planning to stay.*
> *My heart is elated, while my mind*
> *Seeks familiar cues it cannot find.*
> *The joy of newness, the desire to explore,*
> *A new chance at life—can I ask for more?*
> *Oceans away from my comfort zone,*
> *A villainized idea, as opposed to the unknown.*
> *But...*
> *There's a reason the word "comfort" is there.*

I'm allowed to want to crawl back in, where
Sounds of the known embrace me tight.
Less mystery, more history in my line of sight.

I felt untethered, unable to hold on to anything firmly. We tend to give so much importance to our jobs and titles; they become our identity. While I did have the opportunity to work on a few projects that I enjoyed, it wasn't quite the same as having a full-time job with the pay, benefits, and stability I had left behind in order to move and start fresh.

I was now being referred to as a spouse in documents, conversations, and introductions. *Is that my new identity?* I often asked myself.

But then I looked at the man I married—the one who was loving, supportive, and encouraging; the one who had never given me a reason to feel less about myself. While I still felt as if I weren't the captain of my own ship for the first time in my life, I knew I was in calm waters, in good company, and headed toward many possibilities.

One morning, as I sat lost in thought in one of the many beautiful parks in Polanco, a dog wandered up to me. I started petting him, and suddenly it hit me—*Am I not afraid of dogs anymore?* Living in Mexico City, witnessing its famous dog culture, had quietly impacted me. I've always loved animals, but this moment felt different. The dog sat beside me, almost as if he knew something was not right.

Later that day, I decided to declutter my mind and focus on the good things again. I started my morning walks once again, but all I could think about was that profound moment in which I had realized that I could be a dog parent. We made the decision to adopt one, but only after doing thorough research on what it really takes to be a responsible pet parent. Unlike Alexis, I was a first-time pet owner, and I was determined to do it right.

Two weeks later, Alana came home. The moment I held her for the first time, I understood exactly why people refer to their dogs as their children. Becoming a dog parent also opened up new conversations and even sparked some friendships with the locals, as I became part of a vibrant and passionate community.

We were blooming together as a family of three. And soon we'd be a family of four. *While I was building a new life here, I was also creating a new life within me*—another silent achievement that may have gone unnoticed, but one that will shape who I become tomorrow.

Motherhood is a very personal journey, and it is unique for all, down to the last atom of our being. I had always imagined being a mother, but I never expected to experience it so far from home, especially without my own mother nearby. They say it takes a village, and mine was spread across three continents, thousands of miles away. We told each other, "We got this," and I knew Alexis would do everything in his power to be that village—and he did.

Going through my pregnancy in Mexico only further cemented my bond with this country. Our child was going to be a third-culture kid, but first and foremost a Mexican. Tomorrow, when they get nostalgic about their childhood, they will picture Mexico. That's the deepest connection one can have with a place. We owe it to this country to raise our child to love and respect it and to feel a true sense of belonging here.

The months that followed were filled with anticipation and joy as we eagerly awaited our baby's arrival. It wasn't without a few challenges, though. The irony of my doctor telling me not to stress while, at the same time, I stressed about not fully understanding her words was profound. But the care, attention, and quality of healthcare here were reassuring and impressive.

By the spring of 2023, I had been in Mexico for a year, and it was surreal that this coincided with the birth of our son, Nicolás. Among the many things he is going to be, one of them is a reflection of our intercultural love story, our move to Mexico, our diverse ethnicities, and our courage to build and live a life that is no less than extraordinary in my eyes. The same year, both of our parents visited us here, and they echoed the admiration that we had developed for Mexico.

Today, when I travel to India or Spain and say, "We're going back *home*," I mean Mexico. And in my eyes, this is not a status that the country has earned; it's actually the opposite. It was I who was required to go through the process of integration—learning, adapting, and embracing—to earn the privilege of calling Mexico my *home*.

This city in which I once felt like an outlander is today witnessing the first steps, the first words, the first birthday, and every single growth milestone of our son. If that doesn't make it home, I don't know what does.

Our home here is a reflection of our multicultural life. You'll see a piece of Huichol art in one corner, a Basque-country landscape on the other, while a soft Bollywood melody plays in the background, and the fragrance of Mexican rice being cooked with Indian spices fills the rooms. The color of our passports may vary, as do the tones of our skin, but the life we are creating together is painted with the same shade of love.

Our journey began in Mexico City, but we have traveled across the country to learn more about its culture, landscape, and history. From the pristine beaches of Cancun and Los Cabos to the historical architecture of San Miguel De Allende. From the ancient ruins of Oaxaca to the volcano and mountains in Toluca. In the last three years, apart from visiting family in India, Spain, and the UK, we have not felt the need to visit any other country. We are too busy falling in love with the cities, towns, people, and story of Mexico.

You can watch videos and do research online about a country, but the true experience of getting to know a new country, a new culture, a new city lies in the invaluable interactions you have with the people there. As you immerse yourself in a culture that is not yours, you must integrate, celebrate, appreciate, but make sure to never appropriate. There are certain cultural elements that will always belong to the native Mexicans only, and we always remember to respect that.

This home, this family, this life we have built is an extension of my identity—something I once viewed through a very narrow lens. Do I work professionally? Yes, and I love that part of my life. But now I also acknowledge and love the other aspects of my life: the privilege of being a mother and a partner; the joy of drinking a good cup of tea; my poems, which serve as a testimony to the defining moments of my life; my personal style that I only discovered after moving here; my love for the city I come from and the one I came to; the pleasure of speaking the languages I know or am learning; my unfolding story; and my courage.

Today…we live in a neighborhood populated by locals, not in the cosmopolitan Polanco. When I wake up in the morning, the sounds of the city feel familiar. Each time I finish having a conversation in Spanish, I secretly do a little victory dance. I create content to highlight the wonders of this walkable city that has many reasons to be celebrated.

The other day, Alexis asked me, "I don't know what the future holds, but do you see yourself getting old here in Mexico?"

And I repeated the same thing that I said to him when we were starting a new life together, "I do."

What did it take to get to this point? Courage:

> *To step into the unknown and believe that we could figure this out.*
> *To step outside and make a wholehearted effort to integrate.*
> *To make mistakes and learn from them.*
> *To face our fears and not let them dictate our journey.*
> *To reinvent myself and embrace the changes within and around me.*

And, most importantly, the *courage to begin again.*

Mexico City is a world-class city. For the first time in my life, I am living in a place without a timeline or predetermined end date. Mexico City checks all the boxes for me.

Thriving on Change

Joli Divon Saraf

I am a third-culture kid, meaning I was raised in cultures and countries other than either of my parents' and in countries that were not my parents' or my nationalities. Growing up in a diplomatic family, I was no stranger to frequent moves to different countries, including India, Sri Lanka, Canada, and Israel. We moved several times during my childhood, starting (for me) at the age of three. Moving became part of my DNA.

However, there is a big difference between moving when the embassy is taking care of everything for you and moving when you are on your own and have to figure it all out by yourself. And yet, this too I had done on my own numerous times, so I was not unfamiliar with picking up and moving. As an adult, I continued the nomadic lifestyle of my youth. I moved to London to study and work and spent almost six years there. I completed my bachelor of arts degree in history and earned a master of arts degree in international business and management. My passion at the time was all things Paris, so off I went to embark on a new adventure. My time in Paris was short—a mere six months—before I headed to Ottawa, Canada, for a year, followed by four years in Montreal, where I met my husband, Vik, who also happened to be a third-culture kid.

As recent university graduates, my husband and I decided to move to Boston, Massachusetts, for better career opportunities and to escape Montreal winters. We lived in Boston for almost sixteen years, which felt like a lifetime since it was the longest time I had lived in any one country up to that point. It was not in our plans to live so long in Boston; we moved there knowing it was not long term. We were always waiting for the right opportunity to move again. COVID brought just that. We never planned for Mexico to be our next destination, but it turned out to be the best thing that ever happened to us as a family.

Let me take a step back. I had never travelled to Mexico, except for one trip with a friend in 2002 to Club Med Cancun when I was in my twenties, before I was married. That doesn't really count as visiting and getting to know Mexico. While living in Boston, most of our leisure travels were trips to Western Europe and the Middle East to visit family. Mexico was just not on our radar as a holiday destination.

Kim, one of my best friends from my London days, continued living there when I moved to North America. She invited me numerous times to travel with her to San Miguel de Allende during the Christmas holidays. Her parents had retired and moved there from Canada more than twenty years before. Unfortunately, that never panned out because, while Kim was traveling from Europe to Mexico, we were going from Boston to Europe and the Middle East, usually either to Israel or the Netherlands where my parents lived or to Bahrain where my in-laws resided.

During the first months of COVID in 2020, when my husband and I were both working remotely, I wanted to find a warm place to travel to for a couple of months during the winter. As most countries were "closed," we could not travel to our usual destinations. I remembered that Kim's parents lived in San Miguel de Allende, so I looked it up because I knew nothing about San Miguel. It looked like a great option—a stunning UNESCO World Heritage Site with so much culture, history, and perfect weather. So in the summer of 2020, we planned our COVID getaway to spend the coldest Boston months in San Miguel from December 2020 to March 2021.

Spending a few months in San Miguel during COVID was a wonderful introduction to the beauty, culture, and people of Mexico. It was truly a magical time for us. I met the most wonderful people, both locals and expats alike. We discovered cafés, restaurants, galleries, and parks; we walked every street, every neighbourhood, and took whatever tour was available to us. We felt that we got a taste of what life was like in San Miguel, albeit with fewer crowds; the number of visitors or locals out and about was greatly reduced due to COVID. Other than that, San Miguel was as normal as normal could be during such a trying time in the world; with minimal restrictions, it was mostly business as usual. We were thankful that COVID gave us the opportunity to discover a small sliver of Mexico; we immediately fell in love (with San Miguel) and wanted to make it our home. The time had come to leave the United States.

We decided to take a full year to plan our move. We wanted to do everything by the book. I gave my employer at the Massachusetts Institute of Technology (MIT) one year's notice so they had enough time to find someone to fill my position and I could enjoy one last academic cycle from August 2021 to July 2022. We also needed time to do more research on moving to San Miguel and Mexico in general and to arrange for our temporary residency visas. My husband, Vik, an actuary, also needed time to find a new position in a company that allowed him to work one hundred percent remotely and at least fifty percent from Mexico. He was able to secure that six months before our move.

I had a wonderful career at MIT as the assistant director of the Security Studies Program, Center for International Studies, from 2008 to 2022, when we left for Mexico. It was a very fulfilling career, and throughout my time at MIT, I felt so lucky to work with such amazing colleagues and the best bosses one could hope for. My position was incredibly rewarding. I worked on exciting projects while developing the program, and I met and worked with the most interesting people who were at the top of their fields. I really grew as a person and learned so much during my time at MIT. For me, leaving my job was probably the hardest part of leaving Boston.

To add another twist to the story, when we decided to move to Mexico, we were in the middle of the adoption process to adopt a baby girl from India. We did not have a timeline for when we were going to pick her up, but we did know we would have to spend a couple of months in India during the subsequent year. The trip to India happened in June 2021, and we returned to Boston in August 2021 with our baby girl, Ruby.

As we knew that our plan was to move to Mexico in the summer of 2022, we hired a full-time nanny who was from Venezuela and asked her to talk to our daughter in Spanish as much as possible. This way, Ruby would get a head start in the language, which we hoped would ease her adjustment to the new culture after our move. In addition, when we moved to San Miguel at the end of July of 2022, I enrolled Ruby in a three-week local summer camp; none of the teachers (or other kids) spoke English. I had to communicate with the teachers using Google Translate.

Ruby turned three during her time at the camp. I organised a small party for her at the school and provided two pink Minnie Mouse cakes and other goodies for the kids. It was very special to experience the Mexican traditions for celebrating children's birthdays despite the fact I had not brought a piñata; I was not that organized yet because we had been in San Miguel only a little more than a week!

Ruby was very happy at camp, and the teachers told me that although she responded most of the time in English, she understood most of what was being said. Today, she speaks Spanish like a native, and I think the combination of that head start and her young age made that possible.

Once camp was over, I enrolled Ruby in preschool at an international bilingual school, but due to its inconvenient location, I moved her to a Waldorf preschool, which was one hundred percent in Spanish.

As for me, the year before moving to Mexico I tried to learn Spanish using Duolingo. The foreign language that I learned in school was French, so I did not speak even the most basic Spanish.

When we made the decision to move to Mexico, I didn't really know what to expect. I knew that living in San Miguel full time was going to be different from the few months we spent there during COVID. So when I returned to Boston in early 2021, I went into research overdrive. I overdosed on YouTube videos about moving to Mexico in general and San Miguel specifically. I joined numerous Facebook groups so that I could learn from others and paid close attention to questions about moving, the culture, and the dos and don'ts. I stayed in touch with the friends that I made in San Miguel. There was a lot to do but I already felt that I had a support system. I also researched the criteria for temporary residency in Mexico and made an appointment for our family at the Mexican consulate in Boston three months before our planned move, as we knew that once we got our temporary visas, we would have six months to travel to Mexico and go to Immigration for step two of the process and to receive out temporary residency visa cards.

When we were finally back in San Miguel, our temporary residency visas in our passports, we decided to use immigration consultant Sonia Diaz for the final steps of the residency visa process. Sonia Diaz was highly recommended by numerous individuals in the Facebook groups, and although some people do this part themselves, we did not want to take any risk in making a mistake with the paperwork and with the subsequent appointments. It was definitely money well spent. Sonia Diaz was extremely professional, detail oriented, and responsive to emails, and she met us at Immigration for our appointment. Everything went seamlessly, and the three of us left with our temporary residency cards in hand.

We temporarily rented the *casita* of my friend Kim's parents who had retired to Mexico from Vancouver, Canada. We were invited to weekly Friday-night dinners at their house. They made us feel like family. They were also a really great resource and helped make our transition to San Miguel so much easier.

Within a couple of months of moving to San Miguel, we were renting a charming colonial-style house with extremely high ceilings, colorful tiles, and orange walls. Our neighborhood of San Antonio was a ten-minute walk from *el centro*, and we loved walking everywhere.

I would say that my biggest challenge living in San Miguel was not speaking Spanish. It was frustrating at times because I wanted to communicate or chitchat with locals working in stores, driving taxis, employed in our home, serving us in restaurants, etc. You can definitely get by in San Miguel without speaking Spanish, as it is one of the Mexican towns that has drawn many Anglo retirees over the years from the US and Canada, and today more and more young families are also moving there, so the town does cater to expats.

Meeting people and making friends were not difficult. As a self-proclaimed coffee *aficionada* who likes to start her day at a café, there were many high-quality cafés to choose from, and we became regulars at several of them. It was very easy to chat and meet people just hanging out at cafés. Another passion of mine is fitness, and while San Miguel did not have boutique fitness studios or fancy gyms, just walking around on the hilly cobblestone streets and having access to a small basic gym for strength training and cardio seemed to work.

Everything was fine until it was not. It didn't take long to realise that as beautiful as San Miguel was, and despite the great friends I had made, I was bored. Ruby was at school until two in the afternoon every day, so I had my mornings and early afternoons to myself. Vik traveled a lot to the US, so I was essentially a part-time single parent. After I picked up Ruby from school, there was not much to do. We had the occasional playdate in one of two cafés with kid areas and toys or a garden. There was only one park with a playground. Ruby was still very young, and I had to navigate the cobblestone streets and hills with a stroller, or I had to carry her. I was not happy, but I didn't want to admit it to myself. I wanted to make it work since, after all, this is what I wanted, and this is what I planned for...for over a year.

Everything changed when we decided to visit Mexico City in November 2022 during the US Thanksgiving week. I had heard from friends that Mexico City was a great city, so we decided to check it out. I did my research on what to do and where to stay, and we chose the neighbourhood of Polanco.

We were blown away. The energy of Mexico City reminded me of one of my favourite cities—London—but with better weather. There was so much to do, so many parks, museums, beautiful architecture, restaurants, and cafés, and each area had its own distinct character. I realized how much I missed city living. Mexico City offered everything I could possibly want in a city. Both my husband and I immediately felt that this, not San Miguel, was the city for us.

There was nothing keeping us in San Miguel, so we decided to move as soon as possible. We returned to Mexico City the following month for another mini vacation and for additional reconnaissance. We were able to fully move to Mexico City at the end of April 2023. Unlike San Miguel, I didn't have a support network in Mexico City, but it felt so good to be living in an urban environment, and the transition was easier than it was to San Miguel, despite only having a couple of acquaintances in Mexico City.

I felt happy and at home. I loved my new neighborhood of Polanco. I immediately joined a fitness studio for boot camp and strength-training classes. For me, no matter what is going on in my life, exercise is a daily activity, even if just going on a long walk. It elevates my mood and sets my mind for the day.

Next, I needed to figure out how to meet people and cultivate a social life. As part of my research, I discovered that Mexico City had an International Women's Club

(IWC). Joining it changed the trajectory of my experience in Mexico City. I met the most wonderful women from all over the world. Some were there in a diplomatic capacity with their spouses who worked at embassies, others with private companies; some ladies were married to Mexican nationals, and others had their own businesses and decided to move there. Of course, several Mexican women were also members.

The activities provided by the IWC are endless. If you choose to do so, you can be busy with an IWC event every day of the week. I also joined a women's walking and coffee group one morning each week. I started a YouTube Mexico City lifestyle channel (JK Lifestyle) with my good friend, Kirsten, an American expat who has lived in Mexico City for more than ten years. I also joined a Jewish women's social group and became co-chair of the group in January 2025. While doing all of this, I still met other people and made friends while sitting at cafés and taking Ruby to the playground. However, I feel that, had I not joined some of these social groups and made the initial effort to meet other women, it would have been a harder adjustment for me. Not only have I made amazing friends, but I have endless resources for anything related to Mexico and Mexico City.

Ruby was also thriving. She loved her new school and adjusted easily to her new environment. I enrolled her in a bilingual private school about a seven-minute walk from our apartment. We are about a fifteen-minute walk from Chapultepec Park and only minutes from several others. It was important for me to be able to walk everywhere and only take an Uber to other parts of the city when I wanted to explore or visit friends in other neighborhoods.

I also recently decided to try the Mexico City Metro as another method to get around, considering Mexico City's infamous traffic. I was a little apprehensive at first, but the metro is clean, well-lit, efficient, and it has a women's-only section, which makes you feel safer if you are traveling alone.

I don't want to pretend that everything is perfect in Mexico City. No place is. After living in eight countries and twelve cities, you learn to accept that certain things are just the way they are and embrace them as the culture of that place. I had to learn how to navigate simple things, such as paying bills and handling maintenance issues at home with technicians. Not speaking Spanish made it more difficult. After all, I couldn't just pick up the phone and call businesses or ask questions. At times, I had to have my local friends call on my behalf. One specific example was when Ruby fell through a chair and had to get stitches above her eye. We took her to the children's ER at the hospital, and no one spoke English (except the surgeon), so I had to call a Mexican friend to talk through some of the paperwork and to understand the insurance process.

We still visit San Miguel once or twice a year to visit friends and our favorite spots there. Even though it was not the right city for us to live in, San Miguel will always hold a special place in our hearts for introducing us to Mexico.

Mexico City is a world-class city. For the first time in my life, I am living in a place without a timeline or predetermined end date. Mexico City checks all the boxes for me.

I have taken Ruby to numerous museums, classical music concerts, parades, restaurants, cafés, and other cultural and social activities. My current focus is to keep improving my Spanish and taking advantage of all the things this city has to offer.

Having lived in numerous countries, I truly feel like a citizen of the world. Will I move again? Probably. But I am not in a rush.

Sometimes, the boldest move isn't just changing your address —it's reclaiming your voice in a place where no one speaks your language, but everyone is ready to hear your story.

Lost in Translation

Lisa Michelle Umina

There's a saying, "You are one decision away from a completely different life." I didn't understand this until I looked back to twenty years ago when I made the decision to sell my home and move to Mexico. On the airplane, I remember thinking, *Everything I own and my dog, Milo, is beneath me in two large suitcases.* I left everything I knew, including my family. What I didn't realize then, I also left my voice.

Moving to Mexico was supposed to be a new chapter in my life, a bold adventure filled with possibility. I thought I could embrace the change with open arms. After all, I was no stranger to performing under pressure. Back in the US, I had built a career as a stand-up comedian and an author. I spoke to thousands of people, held audiences in the palm of my hand, and inspired children during school visits. Words were my power, my tool, my identity.

I was in a new country, completely starting over, and it was incredibly humbling; I couldn't even ask for a glass of water or tell someone what I was really thinking because I didn't speak Spanish. Imagine how it felt to sit at a dinner table with my new family, all of them trying to get to know me. I tried. Sometimes I said something, and they just looked at me with those endearing eyes, endeavoring to figure out what I was trying to say. But I saw it in their eyes; they had no clue what I was trying to communicate. And no matter how the words came out, I knew my accent was so off. When I look back—and it's still true today—I have to say speaking the language is one of the hardest obstacles I had to face. I tried schools, private teachers, books. Baby steps, they say, or as they say it here in Mexico, *poco a poco*. But it just wasn't working as fast as I needed it to. I needed to communicate with my wife, her family. At times, it was comical when I tried to join words together to make a sentence.

But in Mexico, words became my greatest obstacle. The Performer became the Student. It hit me almost immediately after I arrived: I was utterly unprepared for how isolating it would be not to speak the language. Back in the US, I had never considered myself helpless. I use humor to ease tension, tell stories to make connections, and charm my way through just about any situation.

Little did I realize that in exchange for my life-changing decision and efforts, I would be adopted into a *very* large Mexican family. Not the kind you meet only for holidays and occasional dinners, but the kind you gather with around the dinner table every Sunday, all fifteen talking over each other at lightning speed while you try to figure out if they're arguing, making plans, or just excitedly discussing *telenovelas*. Spoiler alert: It's usually all three at the same time. Initially, they laughed and talked about so many things, and no matter what they said, they wanted me to be a part of it all. I felt overwhelmed. At first, I felt as if I were an outsider looking in. I wanted to connect with them, to share stories and jokes, as I did with my own family back in the States. But the words wouldn't come. It was frustrating, even heartbreaking at times.

I don't think anyone completely understands the sacrifices we make when we move to a different country. The language and culture are completely different and at the same time exciting and challenging. What do you do when you're talking to your wife or your friend is trying to talk to you and share their feelings, or you're trying to share yours, and it's lost in translation?

I remember to this day how I confused very, very important words like *miedo* and *miado*, which means to be scared or to pee yourself. I needed to learn the language, but it was more than that to me. I wasn't here to pass a test; I was here to be heard, to be understood. Oh, and the faces. I would try to say something and force an accent, but I felt as if I were trying to act out a scene; my personality completely changed, and I didn't even know what the heck I was saying, let alone the person I was talking to. Their confused face as I tried to say it slower or faster just to get my point across.

Learning Spanish came with its own unique set of challenges. Unlike English, Spanish is full of regional phrases, colloquialisms, and double meanings that can trip up even the most well-intentioned learner. I quickly discovered that a misplaced word could transform an innocent sentence into an unintentional joke—or, worse, an insult. The first time I tried to order food at a local restaurant, beforehand I nervously rehearsed the sentence in my head. Then waiter approached my table, I smiled, and said, *"Quiero un pollo con frijoles, por favor."* I was so proud of myself… until the waiter gave me a puzzled look and asked me a question I couldn't understand. I panicked. My brain scrambled to translate, but the words escaped me. I could feel the heat rising in my face as I mumbled, *"No entiendo,"* and gestured helplessly. It wasn't just the practicalities of ordering food or finding a restroom that humbled me. It was the feeling of being reduced to someone who couldn't communicate. For someone whose livelihood once depended on words, it felt as if I had lost my dignity.

Once, at a family gathering with my wife's relatives, I tried to compliment someone's cooking. I wanted to say, *"Está muy rico,"* which means "It's very delicious." But instead, I said, *"Estoy muy rico,"* which translates to "I am very rich." The room erupted in laughter, and I stood there, confused and embarrassed, as my wife kindly explained my mistake.

On another occasion, I said, *"¿Dónde está mi escoba de dientes?"* which means "Where is the broom for my teeth?" The word for toothbrush is *cepillo de dientes*. From then on, I remembered the word, but not without a new layer of self-consciousness. These moments were humbling. I wasn't just grappling with a new language; I was learning how deeply tied language is to culture, humor, and identity.

Over time, though, I began to find small ways to connect. I learned how to ask questions—simple ones at first, such as "¿Cómo estás?" or "¿Qué hiciste hoy?" And as I listened to their responses, I started picking up new words and phrases. My wife's family was patient and kind, often correcting me gently or laughing with me when I made mistakes.

One of the most rewarding moments came when I finally managed to tell a funny story in Spanish. It was silly, but it drew laughter from around the table. In that moment, I felt a spark of my old self—the performer who could make people laugh, even in a new language.

Adapting to life in Mexico forced me to confront parts of myself I hadn't fully appreciated before. In the US, I had taken my ability to communicate for granted. I had built my identity around my words, my stories, and my ability to connect with others. But here, stripped of that ability, I felt vulnerable and exposed.

I missed the comfort of being understood, the confidence that came from performing in front of an audience. I missed the person I had been before—someone who could command attention and inspire laughter with ease. But slowly, I began to realize that my struggles were teaching me something valuable. They were teaching me humility, patience, and the importance of listening. They were reminding me that connection isn't just about the words you say; it's about the effort you make, the openness you bring, and the willingness to keep trying, even when it feels impossible.

I knew that the best way to learn any language was to use it, to wrestle with it daily in real-world situations where there was no option but to try. At first, I zeroed in on mastering the words and phrases essential to the book business. I learned how to talk about contracts, cover designs, editing, and publishing timelines. Slowly, I pieced together sentences, often awkward and incomplete, until I developed what I jokingly called my own version of Spanish—a blend of industry jargon, trial-and-error grammar, and more than a few animated hand gestures. It wasn't perfect, but it was functional. I got by.

But as my ambitions grew, so did the challenges. When I decided to expand and lead a team of consultants in Spanish, my patchwork approach was no longer enough. It became clear that I couldn't just "get by" anymore. I needed to do more than talk about books; I had to inspire, instruct, and motivate. I had to lead. And leadership requires connection. Connection requires communication. And communication? Well, that required me to step up my game—to learn proper Spanish, to understand not just the words but the nuances, the humor, the culture. It wasn't about mastering a language for a test; it was about mastering it to build relationships and empower others.

Despite the linguistic hurdles, my determination to make Mexico my true home never wavered. I didn't just want to exist here—I wanted to thrive, to contribute, to be part of something bigger. That's when the light bulb went off. If I could run a successful publishing company in the U.S., why couldn't I open the doors to Latin American authors? Why couldn't I create a space where their stories could be heard, shared, and celebrated? I know how crazy it sounds, especially considering that I still struggled to hold basic conversations in Spanish. But I believed in the power of stories, and I believed in my ability to figure it out.

At that point, I had been running a successful publishing company for eighteen years. Publishing was more than my career—it was my passion. So, if I was living in Mexico, surrounded by new stories, new voices, and new possibilities, why wouldn't I open my doors to the writers here? Why wouldn't I give them the same opportunities I had given authors back in the States? And just like that, Hola Publishing was born—almost overnight.

It was a leap of faith, a bold step into the unknown. I knew it wouldn't be easy, but nothing worth doing ever is. It was messy, it was humbling, and it was one of the most rewarding decisions I've ever made.

It's kind of crazy how it worked out because right after I made that decision, I met a *luchador*, a wrestler, who wanted to publish his book, and then shortly after, I published a famous journalist from Guadalajara who had a large following on her blog and is now an influencer.

I needed to hire consultants; to do that, I needed to use the Spanish I had learned along the way. It was crunch time; I had two new consultants starting, and I was studying nights to learn how to teach them to be consultants who helped people fulfill their dreams. I was quickly reminded of my accent and saw those familiar faces again looking at me, trying to make sense of what I was trying to say.

I'm not sure how it all finally came together, but after months of trying to teach them, they got it. I remember the exact day when I said something in our Monday meeting, and one of them said, "Can you repeat that?! I want to write that down. I love what you said." I literally heard bells and the "Alleluia" chorus. I rejoiced. *I've finally crossed over. I am understood. My voice is finally heard.*

There's a certain joy in the struggle, in the moments when I manage to communicate something meaningful, no matter how clumsy my words might be. Whether it's ordering food at a restaurant, asking for directions, or sharing a laugh with my wife's family, each small victory makes me feel as if I am one step closer to finding my place here.

I know that for some, learning a new language might not seem like a big deal. Many people visit Mexico without ever feeling the need to learn Spanish. But for me, it was about more than just words. It was about connection, about belonging. It was about reclaiming my ability to share my thoughts, my dreams, and my humor in a language that wasn't my own.

Now, looking back on the last twenty years, I realize something important: I never once thought, *This would have been easier if I had stayed in Ohio.* In fact, I think the opposite. I made it here after sleepless nights of self-doubt, through countless awkward conversations, through every mispronounced word.

Mexico has shaped the best version of me.

I won't say I've mastered Spanish (I still have my moments—just ask my wife), but I will say that every misunderstood phrase, every embarrassing mistake, and every small victory has made this journey unforgettable. So if you ever find yourself lost in translation, just remember: The effort is always worth it. And when in doubt, double-check the meaning of the word before you confidently say it in public. Trust me on that one.

About the Authors

Marina Dailly is a passionate traveler and language lover who is fluent in five languages and currently learning Spanish. Growing up in the eighties, the term "third-culture kid" wasn't widely recognized, but now, as an adult, Marina is embracing her unique identity as a blend of African, American, and European influences. This exploration of her cultural heritage has led her to write children's stories focused on global citizenship. Her latest book, *Knock Knock! On the Doors of Magical Monkeys*, reflects this passion. When she's not writing, Marina enjoys jazz clubs, discovering new art, food, and is passionate about human rights issues that impact our world.

Kirsten Harty volunteers as a member of many organizations in Mexico City. In 2013, she founded Women Fit4Life, a support group for women who are interested in fitness and healthy living. She also enjoys organizing weekly walks and taking Spanish conversation, Krav Maga, and salsa dance lessons. Kirsten has a background in real estate and fashion, and loves to travel and entertain.

A proud mother of two wonderful daughters and wife of a man she deeply admires, **Camila Ifanger** is a woman of new beginnings. Deeply inspired by her mother's strength and wisdom, a former HR executive, Reiki master, numerologist, and spirituality expert, she found in self-discovery the path to her personal and professional transformation. After leaving Brazil and facing profound challenges—including an unexpected move to Mexico and the diagnosis of an autoimmune condition—Camila embarked on a journey of rediscovery. It was through this process that she found her true mission: to inspire and guide women in reconnecting with their essence, purpose, and personal power. Because, in the end, the courage to begin again is the path to discovering who we truly are. Today, as a mentor and partner of https://well-beinghuman.co, a community focused on well-being and mental health, she shares her experiences and knowledge to help others navigate their own transitions with courage and awareness.

Elizabeth Lloyd is the founder and CEO of OJO7, the leading online consumer marketing in Latin America. Based in both Mexico City and San Francisco, Elizabeth is an accomplished Internet entrepreneur with over twenty years of international media and technology experience in consumer marketing. She has a track record of accelerated revenue growth, building online companies from pure start-ups to mature businesses. Elizabeth is also a public speaker, media contributor, and industry association member.

Maria Paula Prieto was born and raised in Colombia and now calls Atlanta home. Married and a proud mother of two daughters, she tries to teach them every day to build a life around the belief that dreams are worth chasing at any age. After years of working in nonprofit and government sectors, she pursued her dream to transition into sports media. A multilingual storyteller with a global perspective, she finds joy in connecting with people's journeys, much like the athletes whose stories she now tells. When she's not working or inspiring her daughters to reach for the stars, Maria Paula enjoys hiking trails with her family, losing herself in music that speaks to her soul, and finding quiet moments with a good book, attending sport events—all while keeping up with her two energetic dogs (one of them rescued in Mexico)

Patricia Pulido is a photographer with over a decade of experience; she specializes in storytelling sessions and photo organization for families and small businesses. With a background in fashion design and business administration, she combines creativity with an eye for detail to craft meaningful visual narratives.

Her greatest passion is traveling to new places with her family, immersing herself in diverse cultures, capturing life's moments through her lens, and discovering new flavors as a true foodie. Having lived in Colombia, the USA, Nicaragua, Brazil, and Mexico, she has developed a deep appreciation for storytelling, especially through street photography.

When she is not behind the camera, she enjoys karaoke, upcycling clothes, cooking on her Thermomix, crafting, visiting museums, working out, and participating in social projects. She is the wife of a supportive and encouraging husband. Above all, Patricia is a proud mom of two amazing and sweet kids, who continue to be her greatest source of inspiration and what motivated her to write her first short memoir.

Maria Fernanda Rodriguez was born in Venezuela more than four decades ago. There, she grew amidst a big family bursting with love. She graduated with a degree in industrial relations and started her career in human resources. She has had the opportunity to live in many different cities—New York, Bogotá, and now in Mexico City— which has honed her abilities to adapt and live with no strings attached. In each country, she has left a piece of her life and, in return, has been filled with a thousand experiences.

Sadia Salam is a mother, writer, and content creator. Born and raised in India, she relocated to Mexico City in 2022 to start a new chapter 8,700 miles from where her life's journey began. A seasoned marketing professional, Sadia's love for storytelling goes beyond work and into poems and social media videos in which she combines her love for fashion and cultural exploration to highlight life in a walkable city. Being a part of the Indian community, which makes up less than 1 percent of Mexico's population, her story is that of building a multicultural life with her Basque husband, their son born in Mexico, and their Mexican dog, while blending into a new culture as a family.

LinkedIn: @sadiasalam
www.linkedin.com/in/sadiasalam

Joli Divon Saraf was born in Jerusalem and spent her childhood travelling the world with her family in a diplomatic capacity. She grew up across the Middle East, Asia, and North America, embracing a global perspective from an early age. Continuing her nomadic lifestyle as an adult, she lived and studied in Europe before eventually returning to North America and settling in Boston, Massachusetts. For over fourteen years, Joli served as the assistant director of the Security Studies Program at the Massachusetts Institute of Technology (MIT) in Cambridge, Massachusetts. In 2022, she embarked on a new adventure, relocating to Mexico with her husband and daughter.

Lisa Michelle Umina is an award-winning author, publisher, speaker, and podcast host. As the founder and CEO of Halo Publishing International, she has helped bring over 3,000 titles to life since 2002. Lisa is the author of several acclaimed books, including *Milo and the Green Wagon* and the anthology *Shattered Silence: Stories of Loss and Healing*. With more than two decades of experience in the publishing industry, she is a passionate mentor to authors around the world, offering expert guidance on writing, marketing, and self-publishing. Lisa also hosts the Award-Winning Authors podcast, where she spotlights powerful voices and shares insights from across the literary landscape.

Her work and collaborations with industry leaders such as Ingram Book Group, the Independent Book Publishers Association (IBPA), and Publishers Weekly have solidified Lisa's reputation as a respected leader in the publishing industry, continually elevating the standards and reach of independent publishing on a global scale.

Halo
PUBLISHING
INTERNATIONAL

Founded in 2002, Halo Publishing International is a hybrid publisher dedicated to helping authors around the world bring their stories to life. We offer flexible and affordable publishing options that blend the best of traditional and self-publishing. Our services include professional editing, custom cover design, formatting, printing, global distribution, and marketing support.

Whether you're writing fiction, nonfiction, children's books, or faith-based works, our mission is to empower you to publish with quality, integrity, and confidence.

Follow us on our social media
HaloPublishingInternational

To know more about Halo Publishing International please visit
www.halopublishing.com

www.ingramcontent.com/pod-product-compliance
Lightning Source LLC
LaVergne TN
LVHW021455080426
835509LV00018B/2294